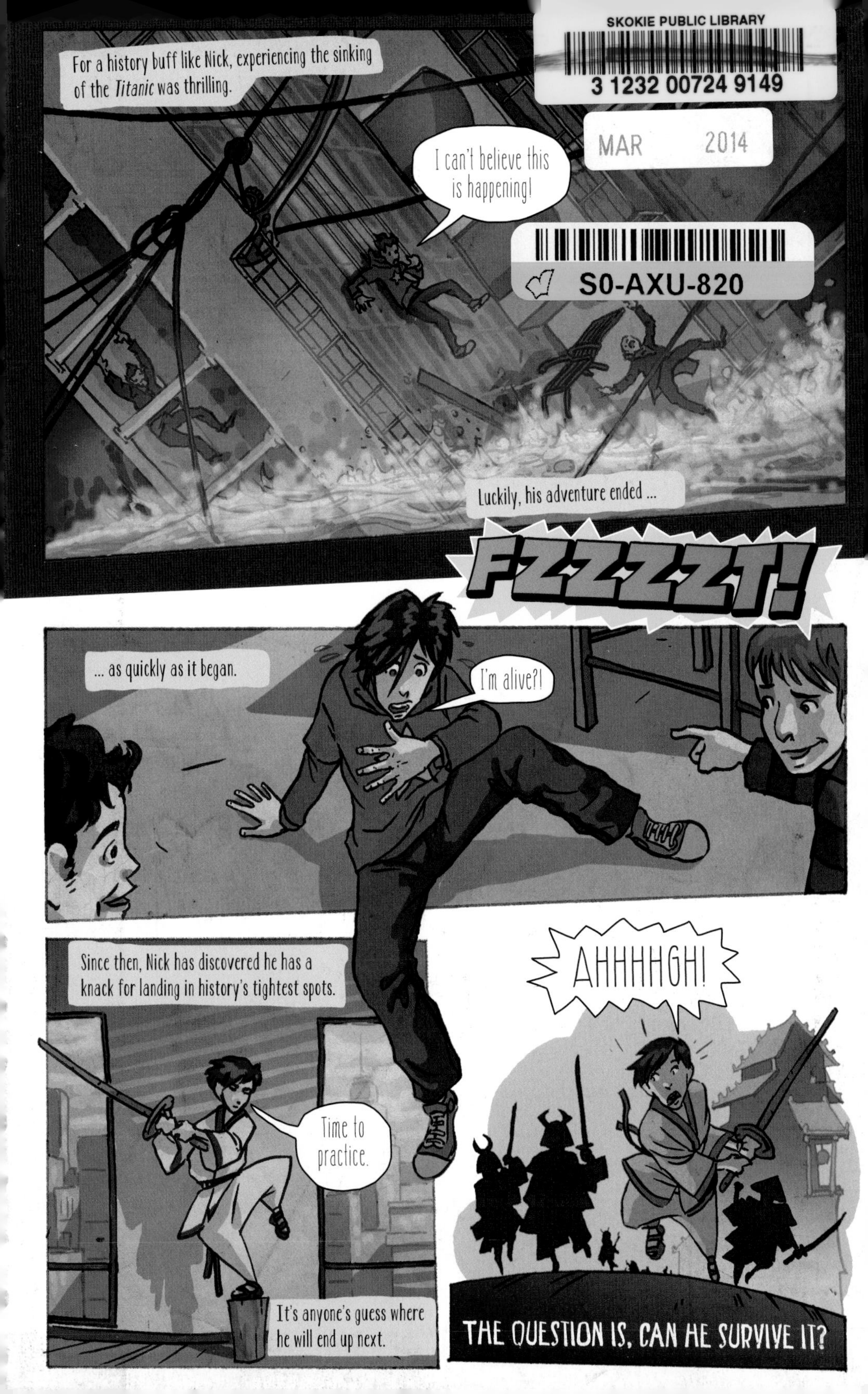
For a history buff like Nick, experiencing the sinking of the *Titanic* was thrilling.
I can't believe this is happening!
Luckily, his adventure ended ...
FZZZZT!
... as quickly as it began.
I'm alive?!
Since then, Nick has discovered he has a knack for landing in history's tightest spots.
AHHHHGH!
Time to practice.
It's anyone's guess where he will end up next.
THE QUESTION IS, CAN HE SURVIVE IT?

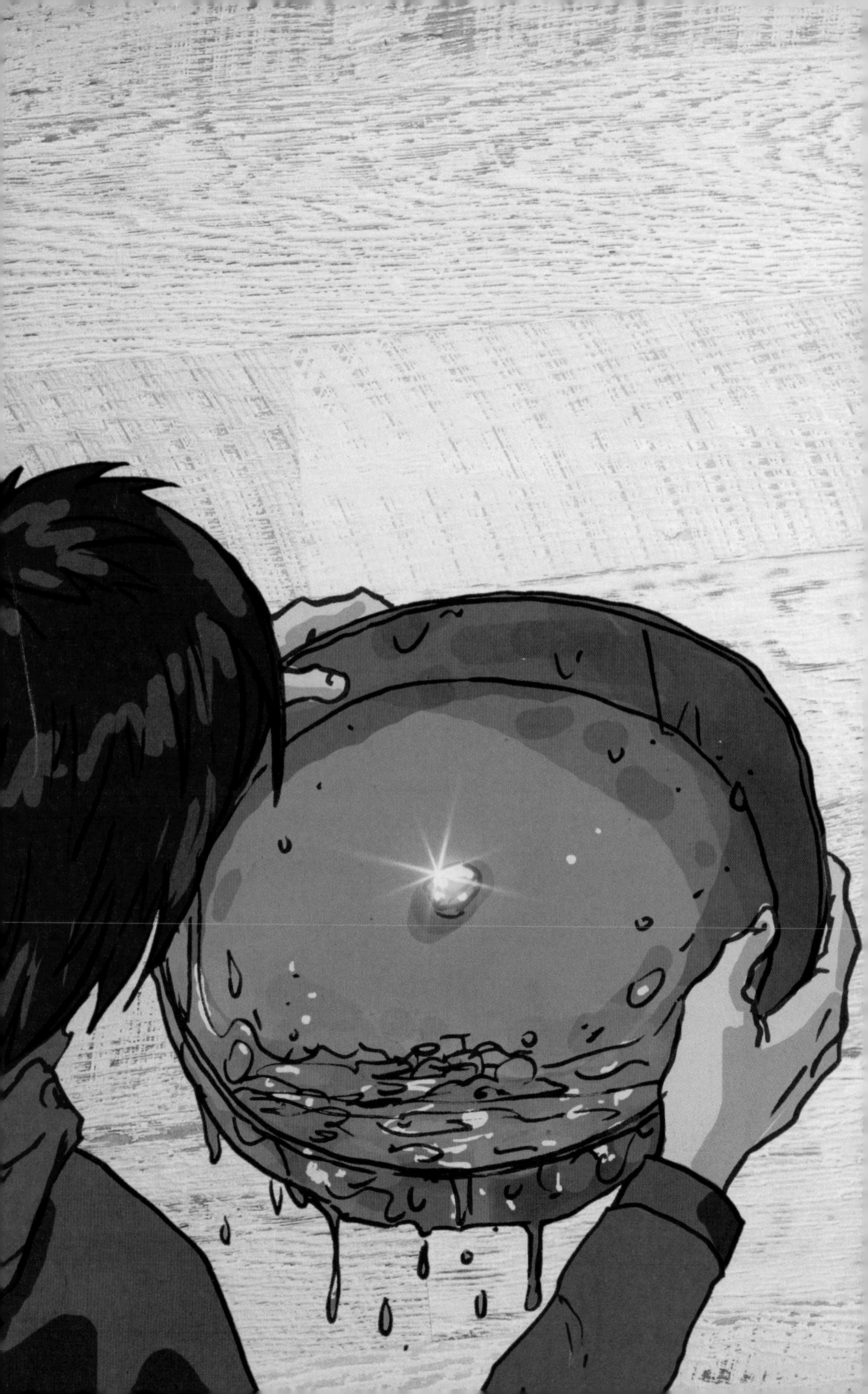

Nickolas Flux HISTORY CHRONICLES

STAKE A CLAIM!

NICKOLAS FLUX and the California Gold Rush

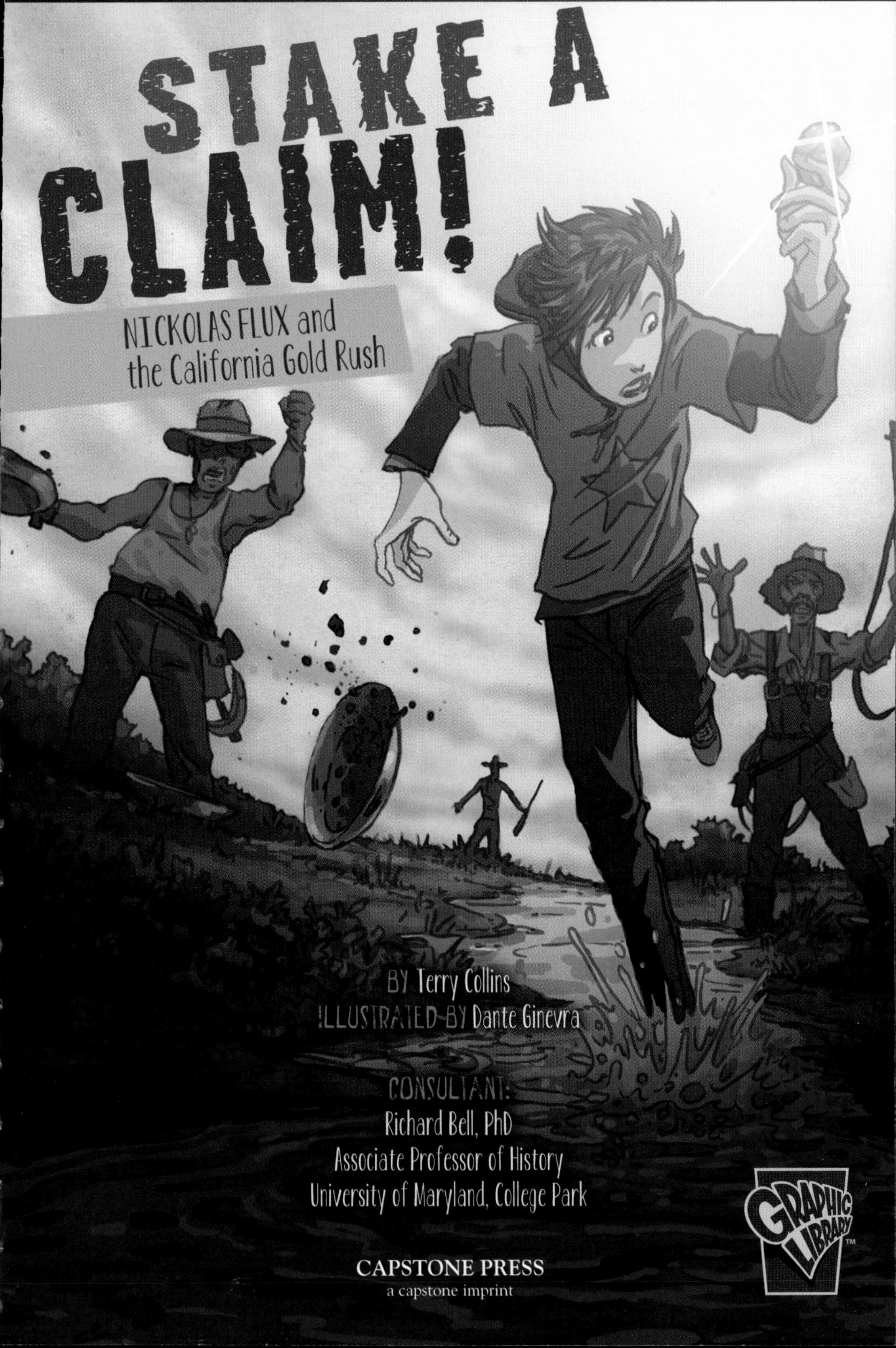

BY Terry Collins

ILLUSTRATED BY Dante Ginevra

CONSULTANT:
Richard Bell, PhD
Associate Professor of History
University of Maryland, College Park

GRAPHIC LIBRARY™

CAPSTONE PRESS
a capstone imprint

Graphic Library is published by Capstone Press,
1710 Roe Crest Drive, North Mankato, Minnesota 56003
www.capstonepub.com

Library of Congress Cataloging-in-Publication Data
Collins, Terry (Terry Lee)
  Stake a claim! : Nickolas Flux and the California Gold Rush / by Terry
Collins ; illustrated by Dante Ginevra.
     pages cm.—(Graphic library. Nickolas Flux history chronicles)
  Summary: "In graphic novel format, follows the adventures of Nickolas
Flux as he travels back in time and must survive the California gold rush"—
Provided by publisher.
  Includes bibliographical references and index.
  ISBN 978-1-4765-3944-7 (library binding)
  ISBN 978-1-4765-5148-7 (paperback)
  ISBN 978-1-4765-6005-2 (eBook PDF)
1. California—Gold discoveries—Juvenile literature. 2. California—
History—1846–1850—Juvenile literature. 3. Frontier and pioneer life—
California—Juvenile literature. 4. California—Gold discoveries—Comic
books, strips, etc. 5. California—History—1846–1850—Comic books, strips,
etc. 6. Frontier and pioneer life—California—Comic books, strips, etc. I.
Ginevra, Dante, 1976– illustrator. II. Title.
  F865.C65 2014
  979.4'03—dc23   2013028002

Photo Credits:
Design Elements: Shutterstock (backgrounds)

Editor's note:
Direct quotations, noted in red type, appear on the following pages:
Page 11, from *Gold Dust and Gunsmoke: Tales of Gold Rush Outlaws,
Gunfighters, Lawmen, and Vigilantes* by John Boessenecker
(New York: John Wiley, 1999).

Page 13, from *Volunteer Forty-Niners: Tennesseans and the California Gold
Rush* by Walter T. Durham (Nashville: Vanderbilt University Press, 1997).

EDITOR
Christopher L. Harbo

DESIGNER
Ashlee Suker

ART DIRECTOR
Nathan Gassman

PRODUCTION SPECIALIST
Kathy McColley

Printed in the United States of America in Stevens Point, Wisconsin.
092013   007767WZS14

TABLE OF CONTENTS

INTRODUCING ...

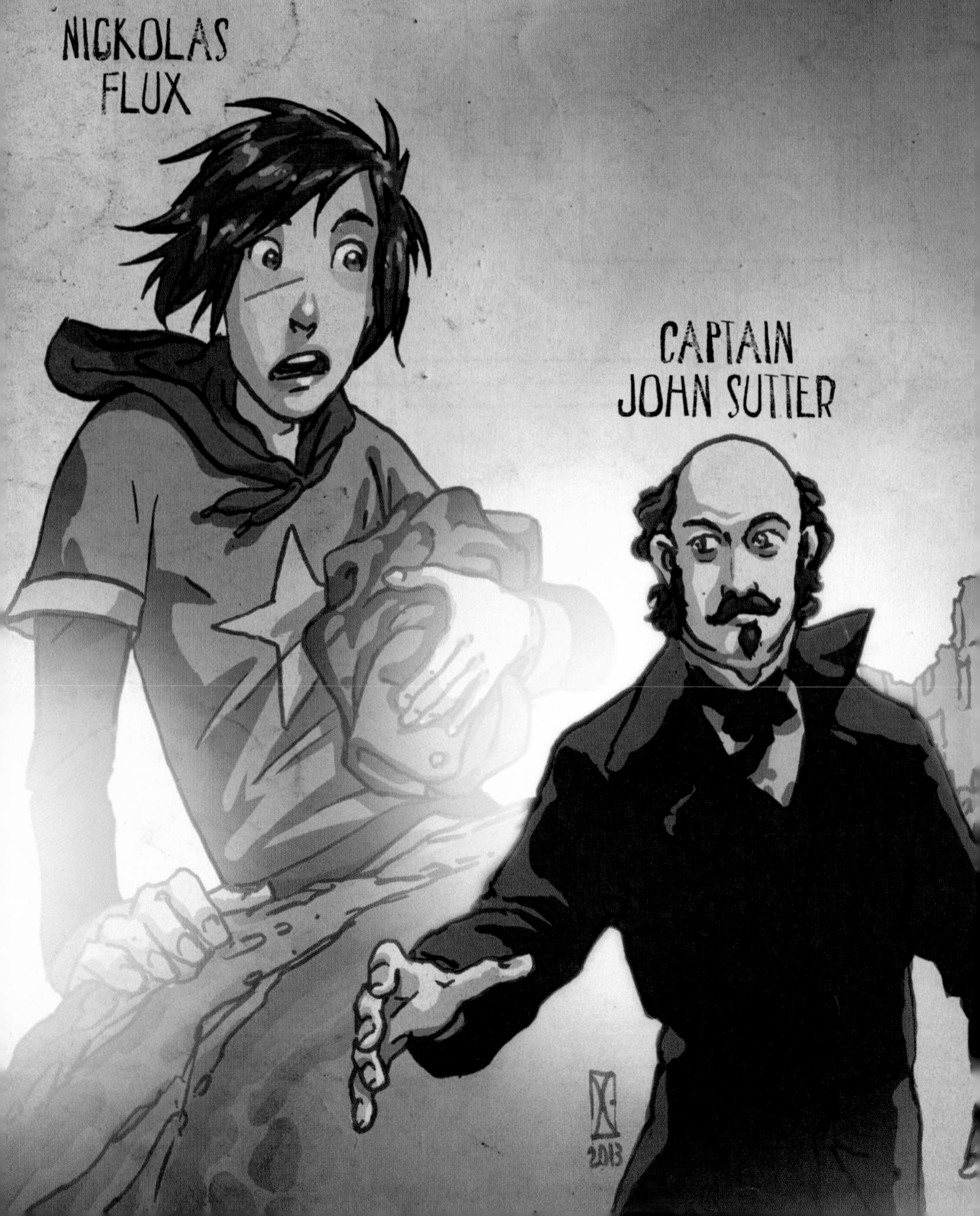
NICKOLAS FLUX
CAPTAIN JOHN SUTTER

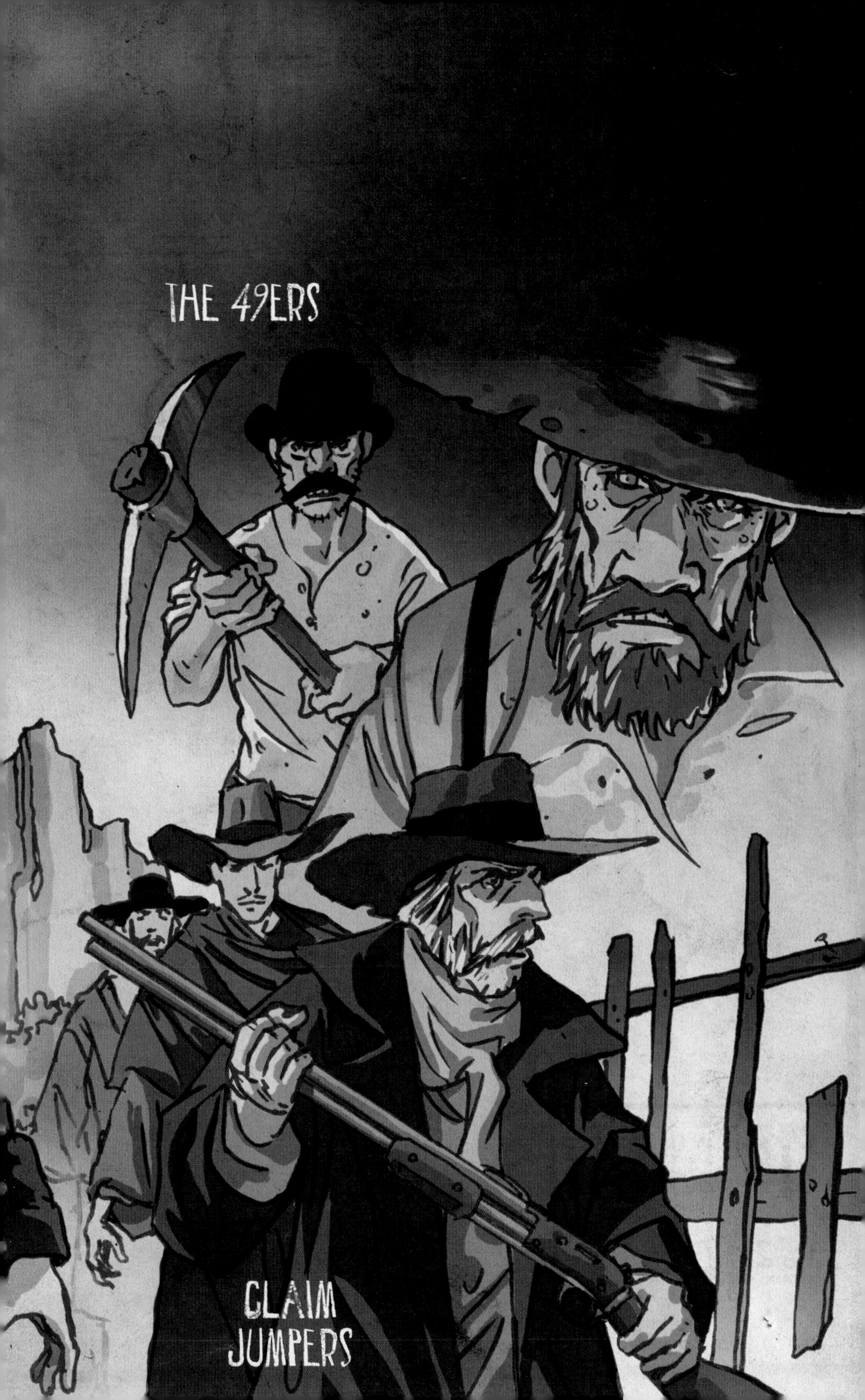
THE 49ERS
CLAIM
JUMPERS

CHAPTER ONE
A GOLDEN GLOW

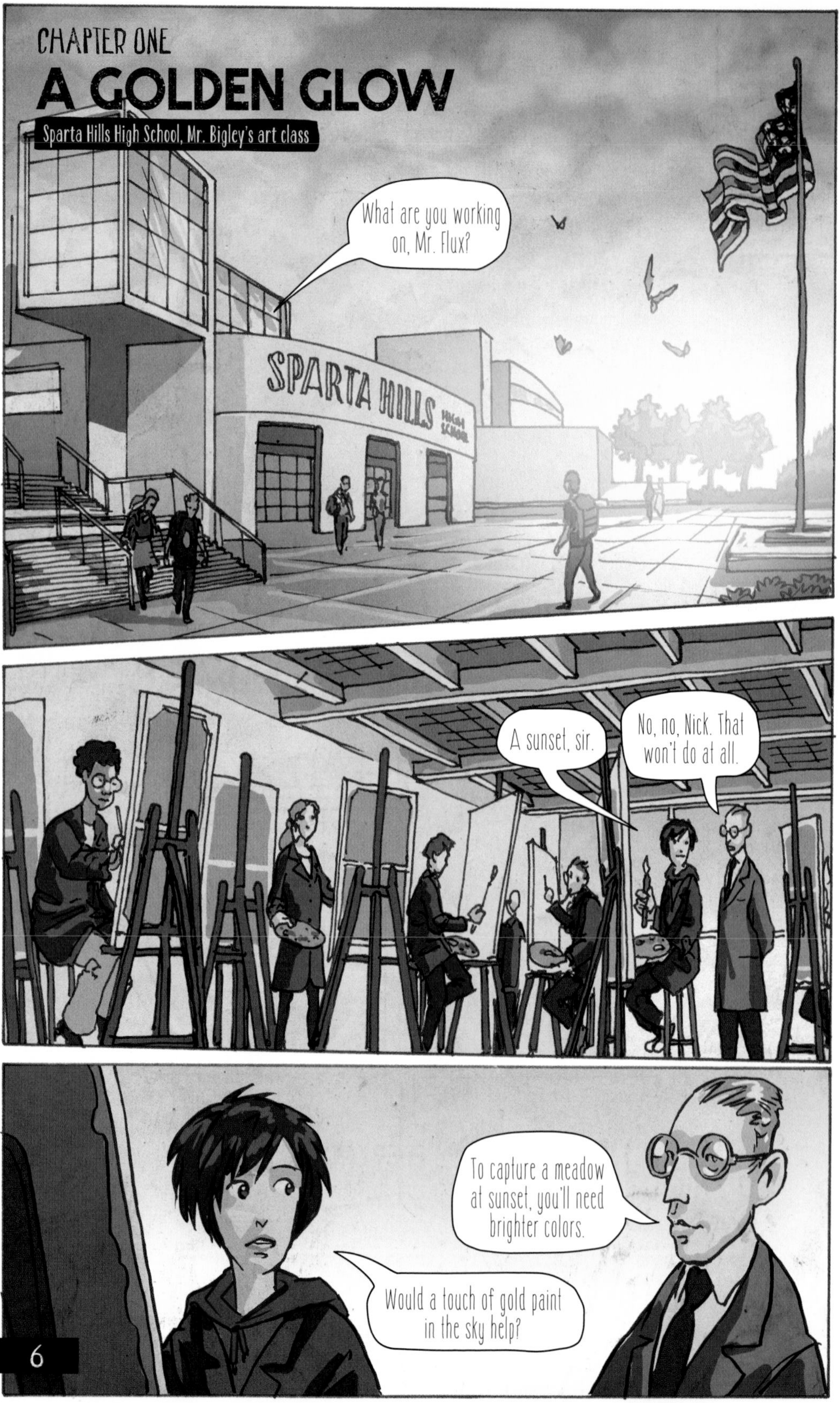
Sparta Hills High School, Mr. Bigley's art class
What are you working on, Mr. Flux?
SPARTA HILLS HIGH SCHOOL
A sunset, sir.
No, no, Nick. That won't do at all.
To capture a meadow at sunset, you'll need brighter colors.
Would a touch of gold paint in the sky help?

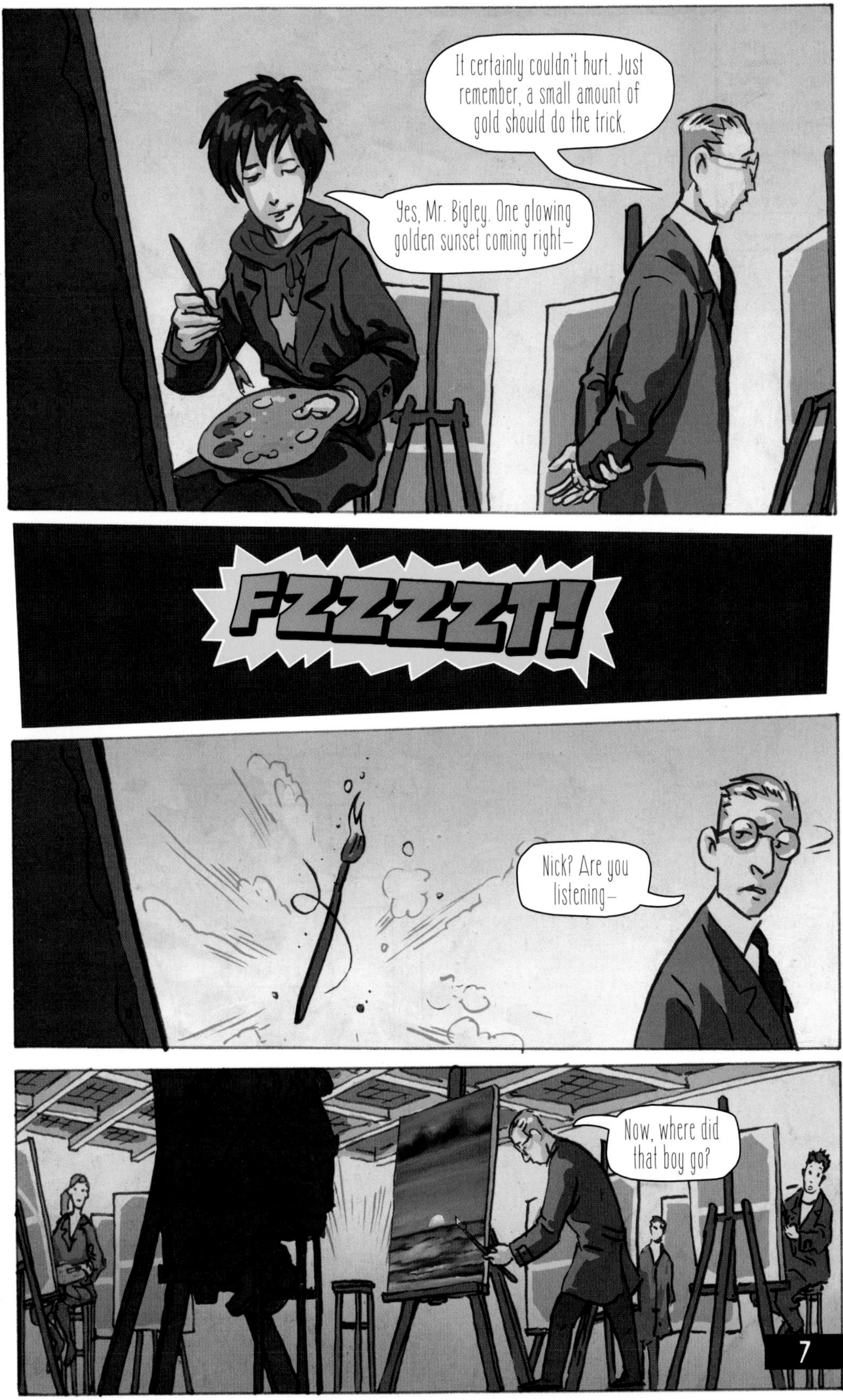
It certainly couldn't hurt. Just remember, a small amount of gold should do the trick.
Yes, Mr. Bigley. One glowing golden sunset coming right–
FZZZZT!
Nick? Are you listening–
Now, where did that boy go?

CHAPTER TWO
GO WEST, YOUNG FLUX

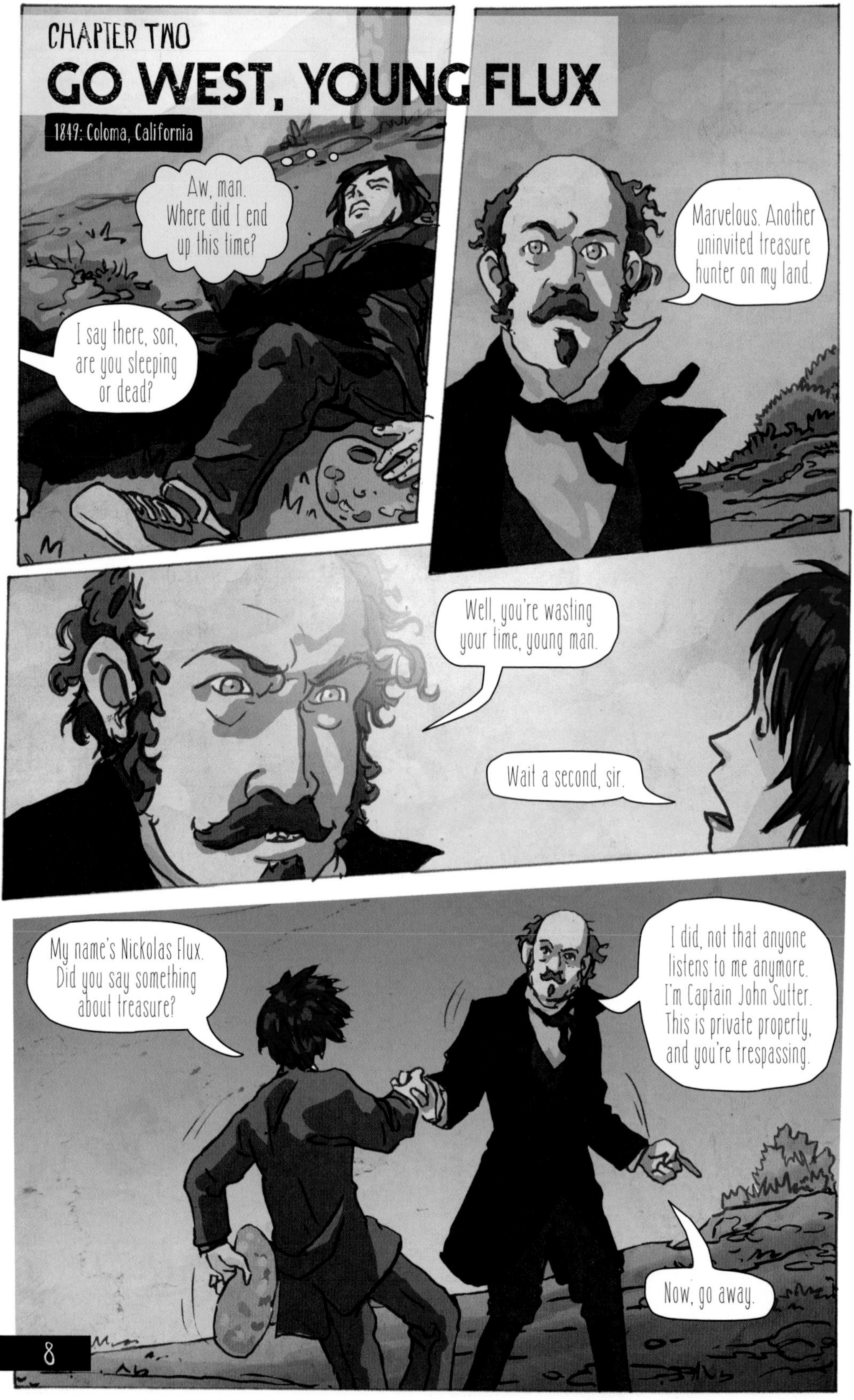
1849: Coloma, California
Aw, man. Where did I end up this time?
I say there, son, are you sleeping or dead?
Marvelous. Another uninvited treasure hunter on my land.
Well, you're wasting your time, young man.
Wait a second, sir.
My name's Nickolas Flux. Did you say something about treasure?
I did, not that anyone listens to me anymore. I'm Captain John Sutter. This is private property, and you're trespassing.
Now, go away.

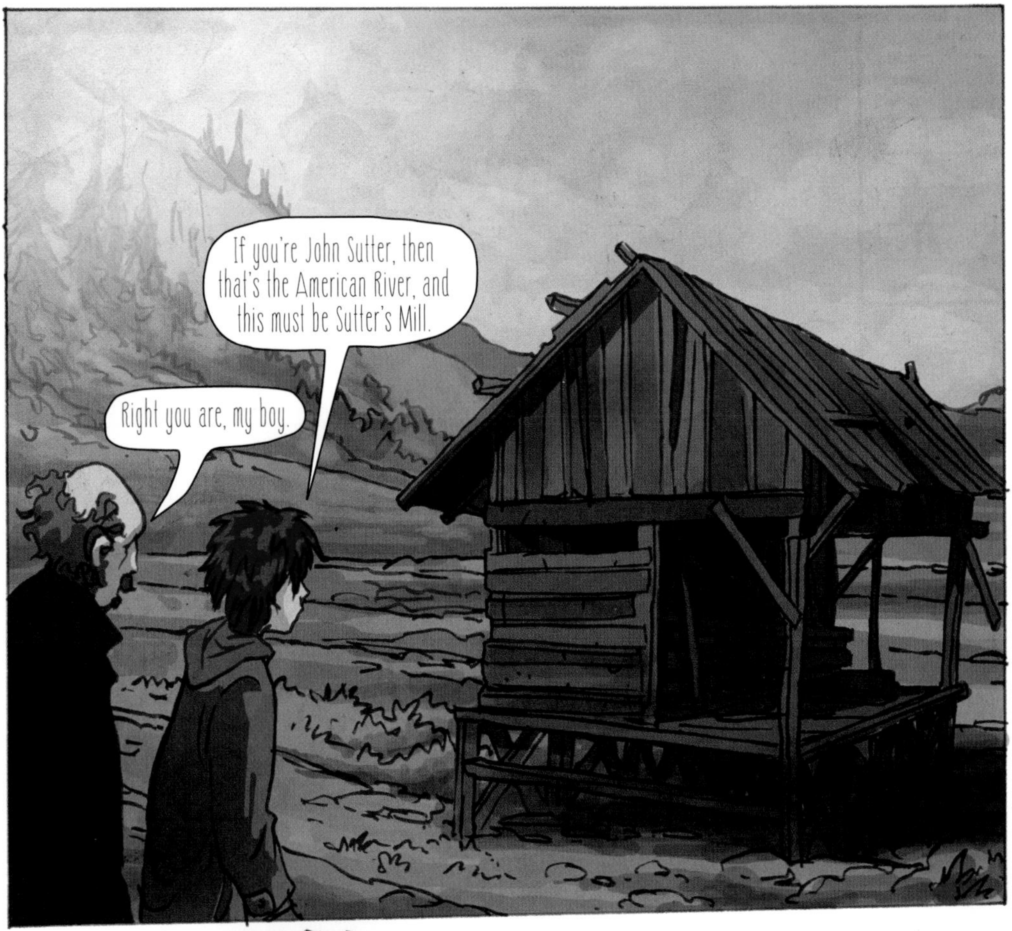

If you're John Sutter, then that's the American River, and this must be Sutter's Mill.
Right you are, my boy.

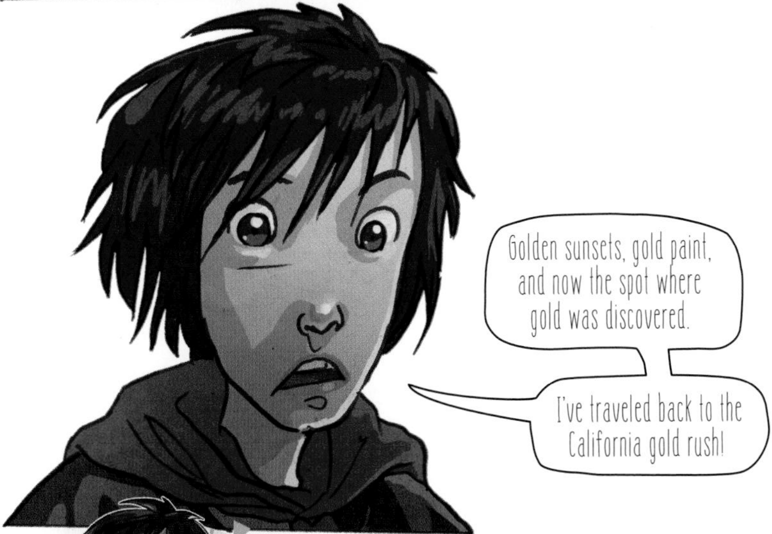

Golden sunsets, gold paint, and now the spot where gold was discovered.
I've traveled back to the California gold rush!

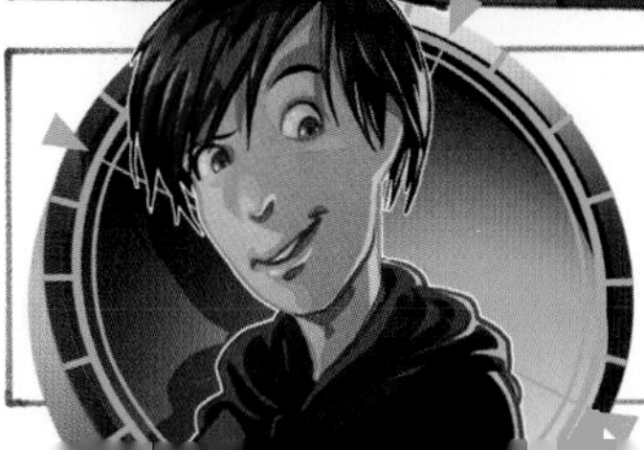

FLUX FACT

Captain John Sutter planned on building a community to be called New Switzerland. The sawmill was needed for lumber to create the new town.

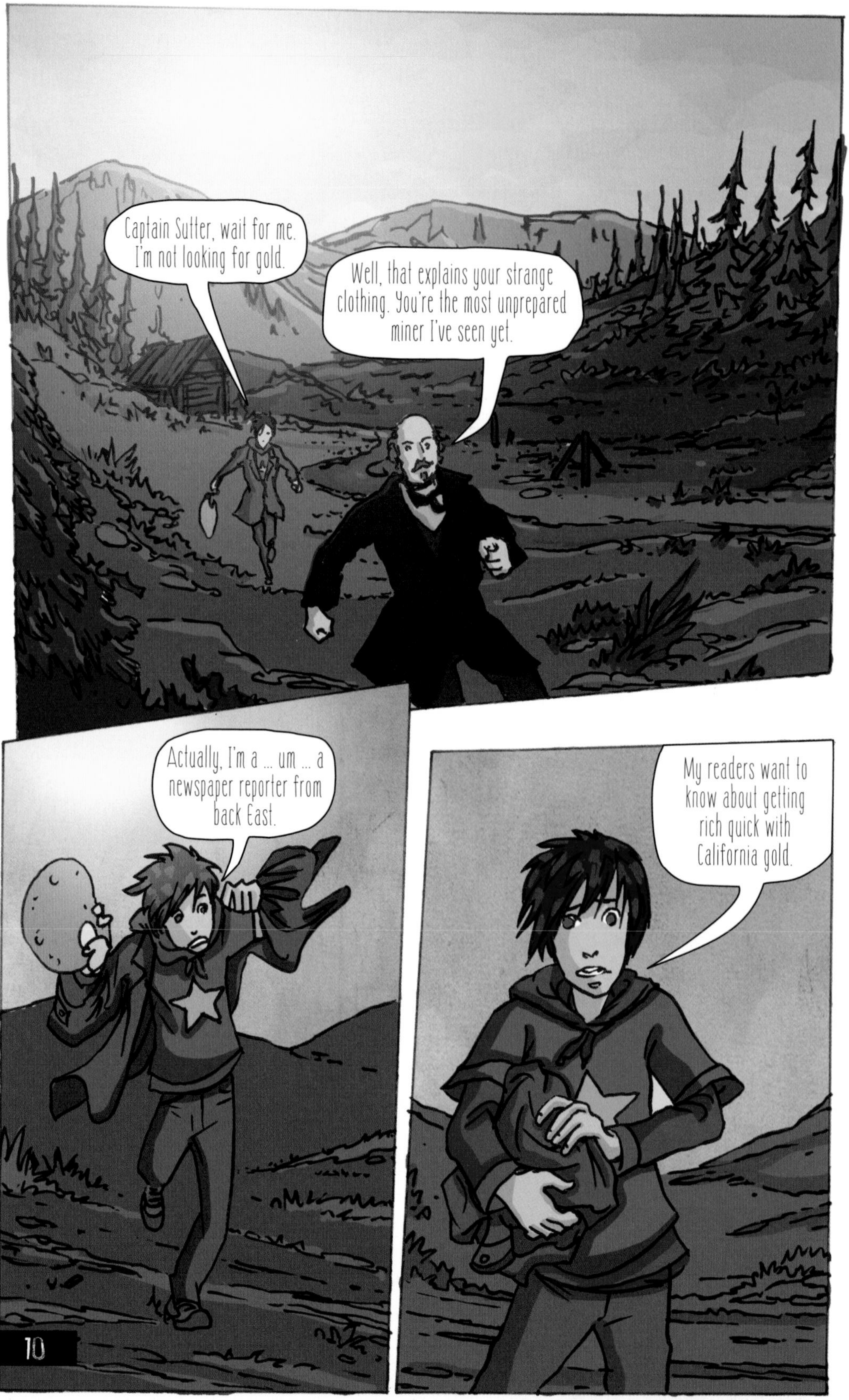

Captain Sutter, wait for me. I'm not looking for gold.
Well, that explains your strange clothing. You're the most unprepared miner I've seen yet.
Actually, I'm a ... um ... a newspaper reporter from back East.
My readers want to know about getting rich quick with California gold.

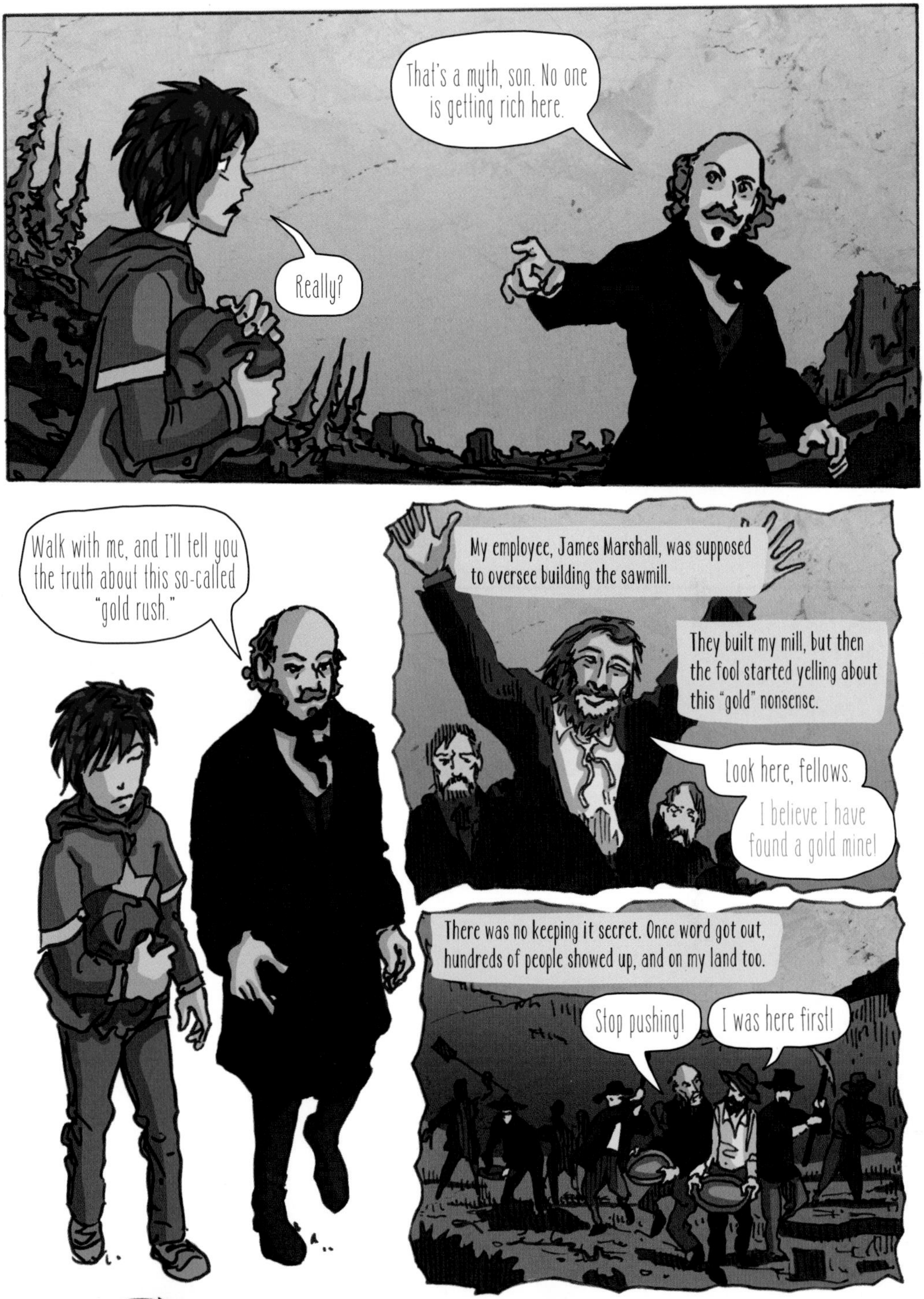
That's a myth, son. No one is getting rich here.
Really?
Walk with me, and I'll tell you the truth about this so-called "gold rush."
My employee, James Marshall, was supposed to oversee building the sawmill.
They built my mill, but then the fool started yelling about this "gold" nonsense.
Look here, fellows.
I believe I have found a gold mine!
There was no keeping it secret. Once word got out, hundreds of people showed up, and on my land too.
Stop pushing!
I was here first!

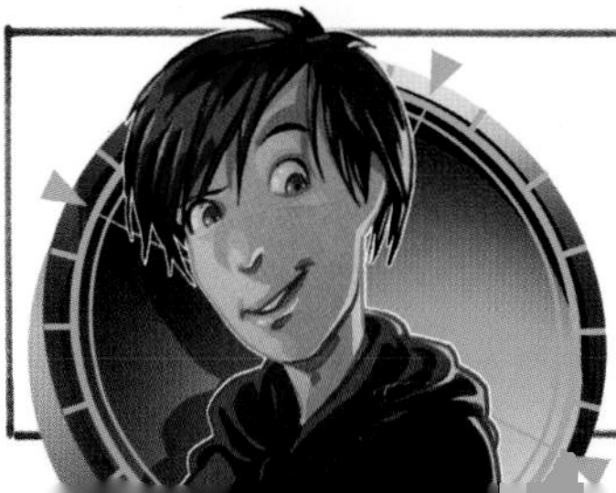

FLUX FACT

On January 24, 1848, James Marshall noticed several shiny pebbles in a runoff ditch from the mill. He took the golden nuggets to the nearby town that would become San Francisco. The gold rush was on.

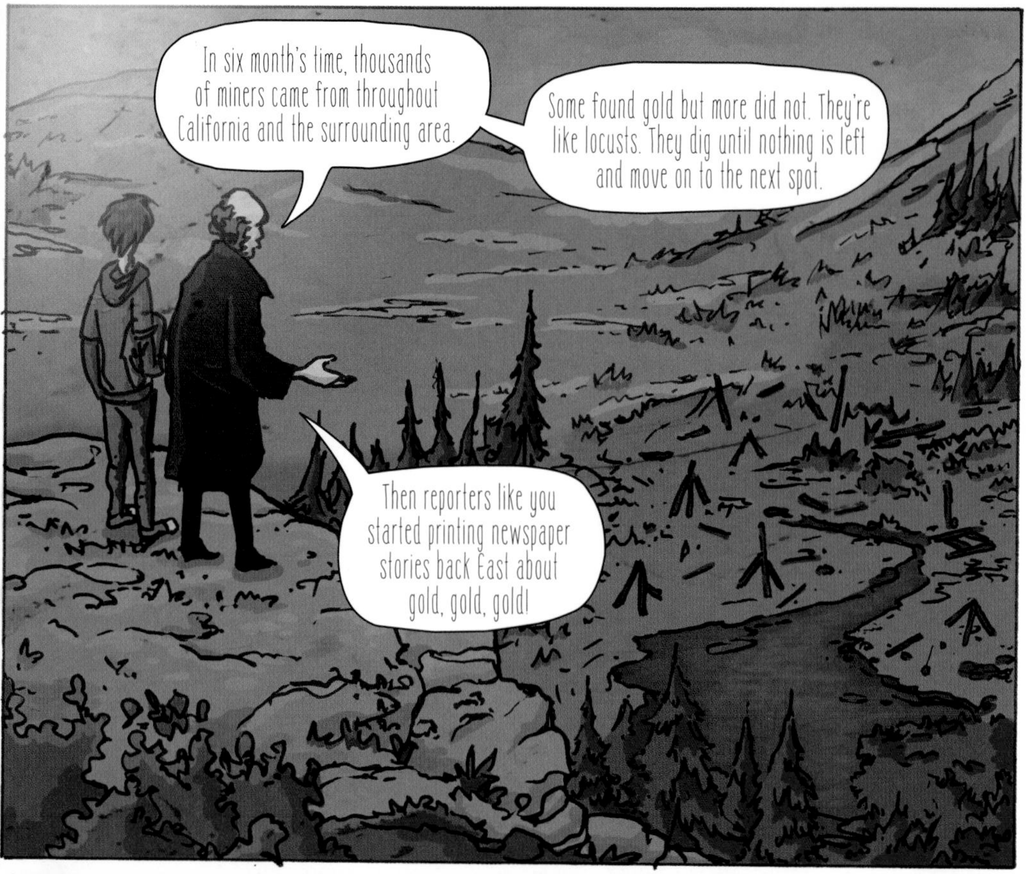
In six month's time, thousands of miners came from throughout California and the surrounding area.
Some found gold but more did not. They're like locusts. They dig until nothing is left and move on to the next spot.
Then reporters like you started printing newspaper stories back East about gold, gold, gold!

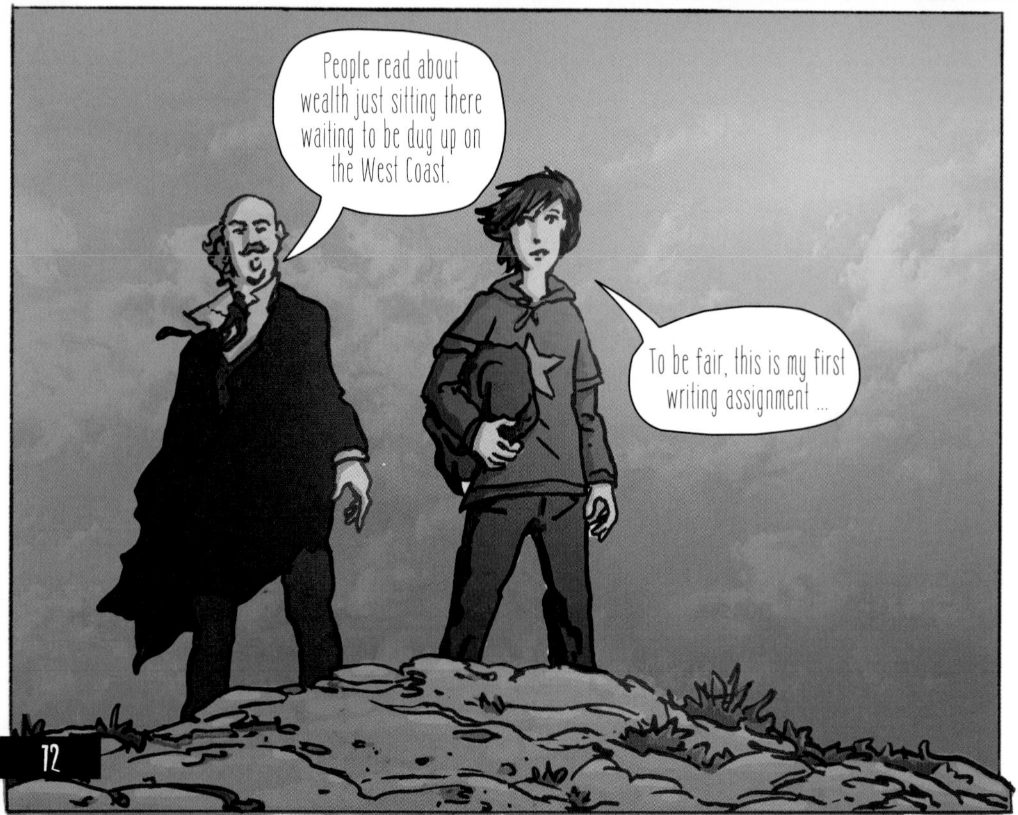
People read about wealth just sitting there waiting to be dug up on the West Coast.
To be fair, this is my first writing assignment ...

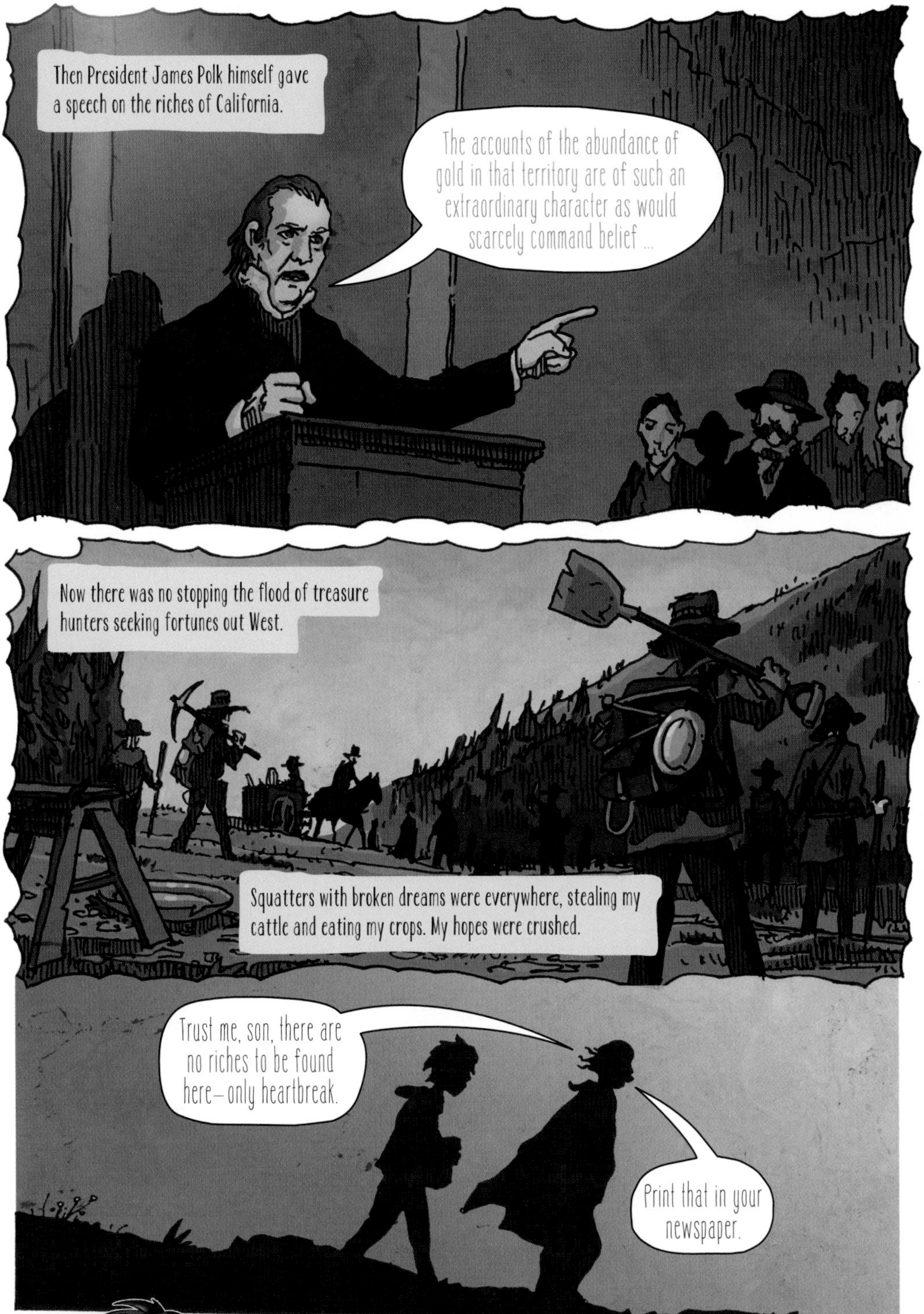
Then President James Polk himself gave a speech on the riches of California.
The accounts of the abundance of gold in that territory are of such an extraordinary character as would scarcely command belief ...
Now there was no stopping the flood of treasure hunters seeking fortunes out West.
Squatters with broken dreams were everywhere, stealing my cattle and eating my crops. My hopes were crushed.
Trust me, son, there are no riches to be found here– only heartbreak.
Print that in your newspaper.

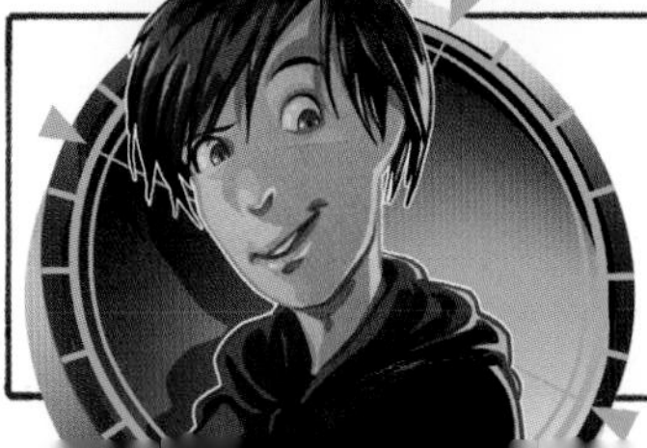

FLUX FACT

Millions of people read President Polk's speech about gold in California on December 5, 1848. In the next four years, the number of people mining for gold in California jumped from about 4,000 to 100,000.

CHAPTER THREE

HANGING WITH THE 49ERS

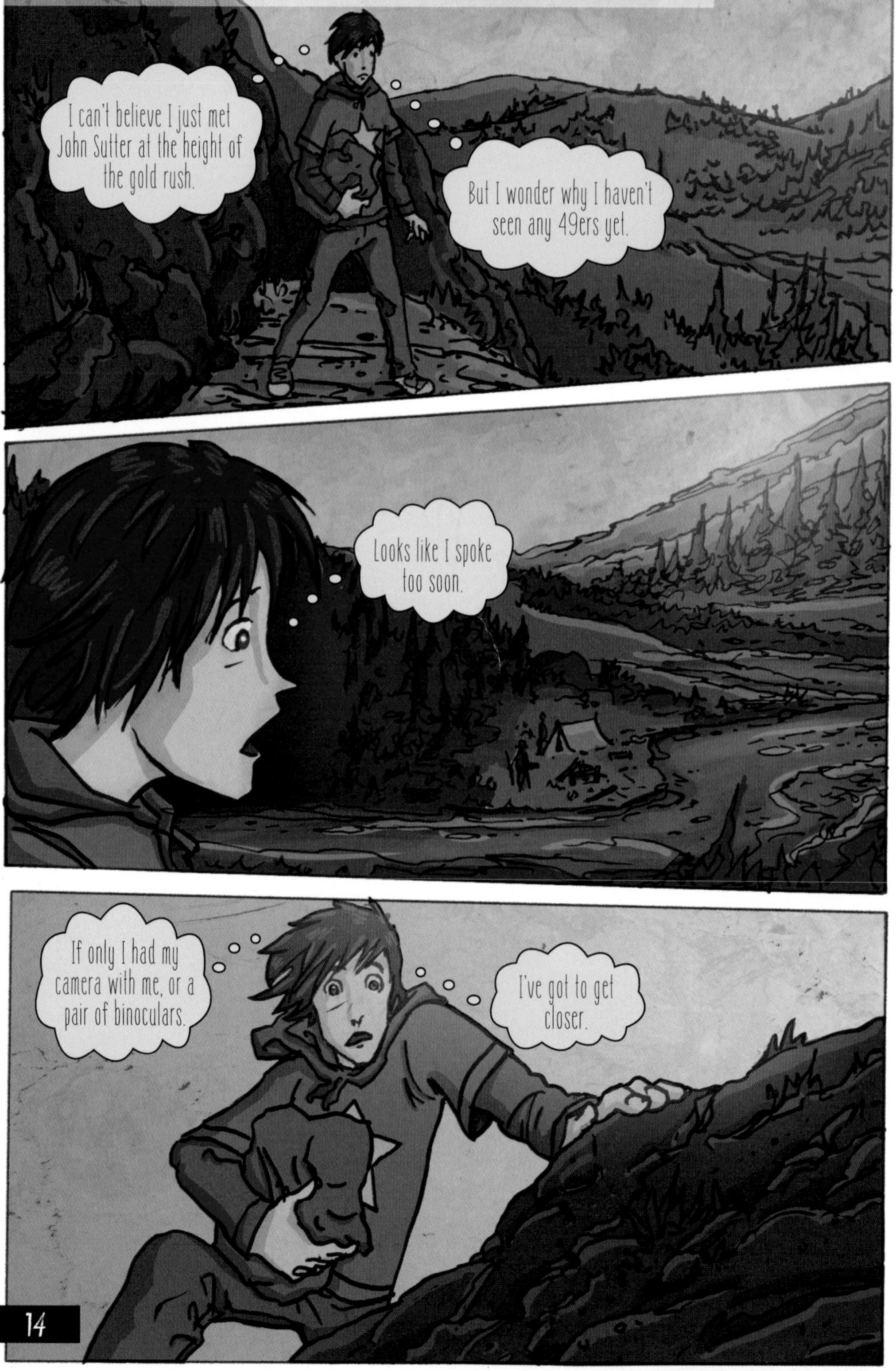

I can't believe I just met John Sutter at the height of the gold rush.
But I wonder why I haven't seen any 49ers yet.
Looks like I spoke too soon.
If only I had my camera with me, or a pair of binoculars.
I've got to get closer.

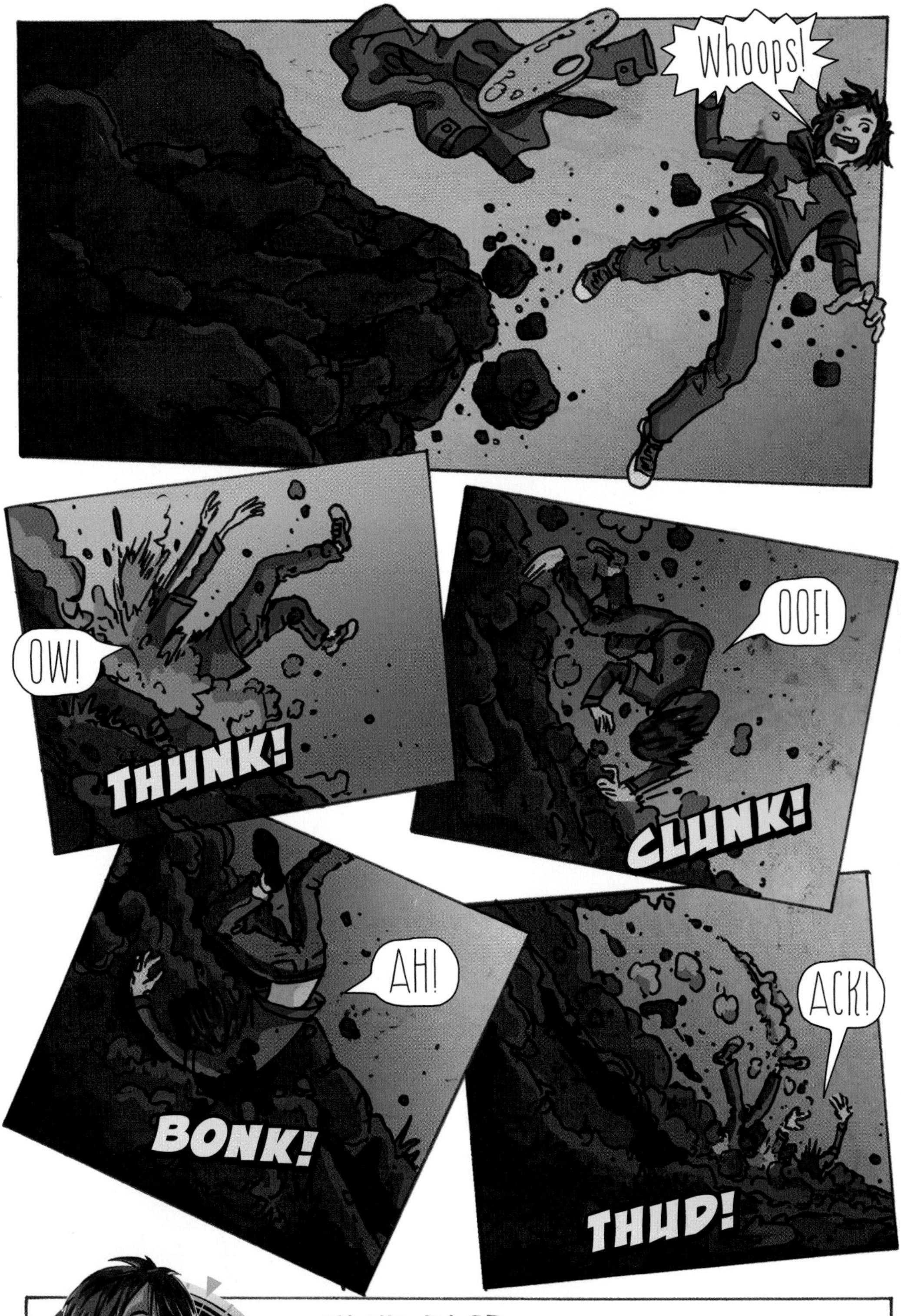
Whoops!
OW!
THUNK!
OOF!
CLUNK!
AH!
BONK!
ACK!
THUD!

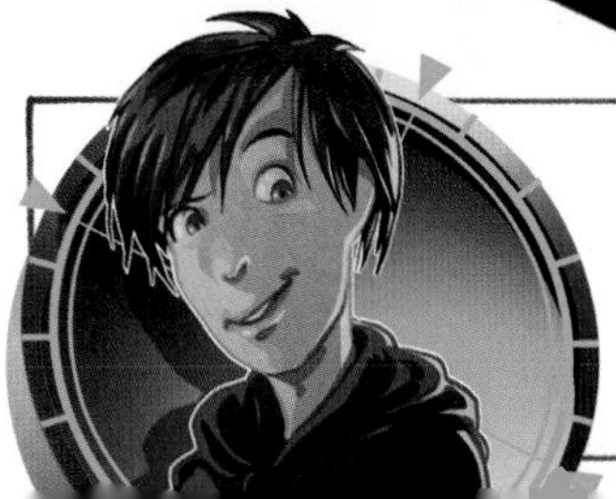

FLUX FACT

By January 1849, the gold rush was in full swing. As a result, the thousands who came to California were called the Forty-Niners (49ers).

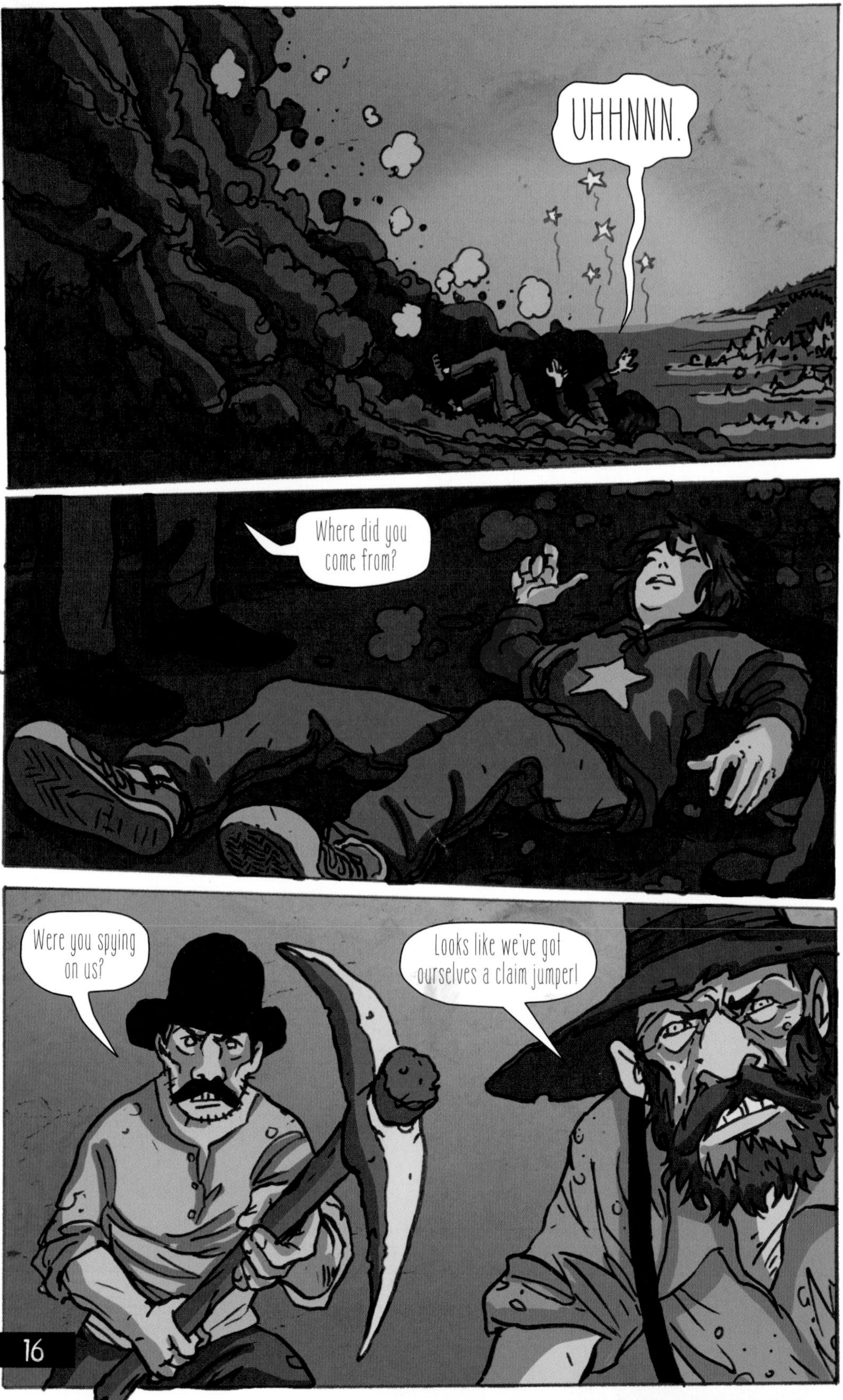
UHHNNN.
Where did you come from?
Were you spying on us?
Looks like we've got ourselves a claim jumper!

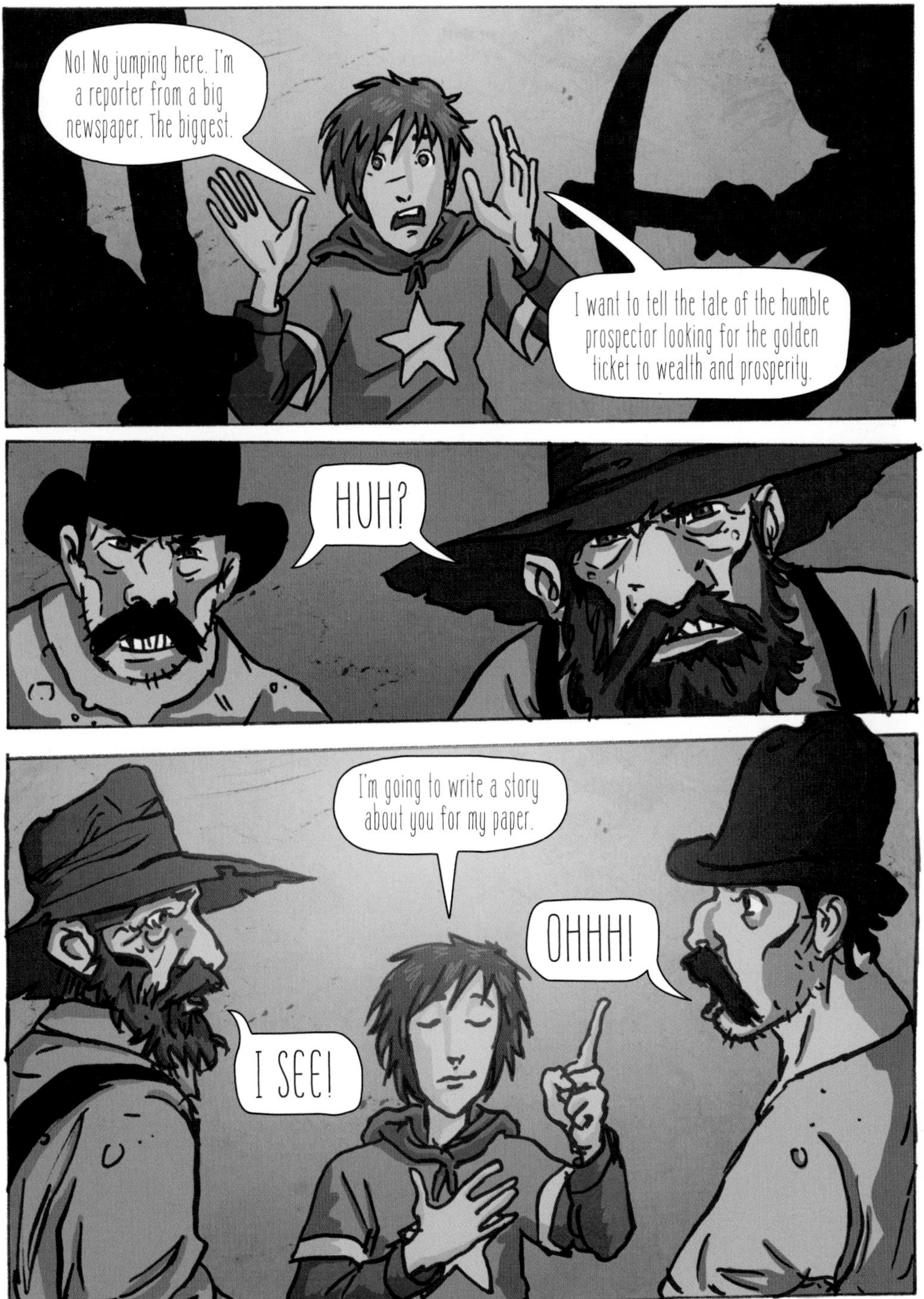
No! No jumping here. I'm a reporter from a big newspaper. The biggest.
I want to tell the tale of the humble prospector looking for the golden ticket to wealth and prosperity.
HUH?
I'm going to write a story about you for my paper.
I SEE!
OHHH!

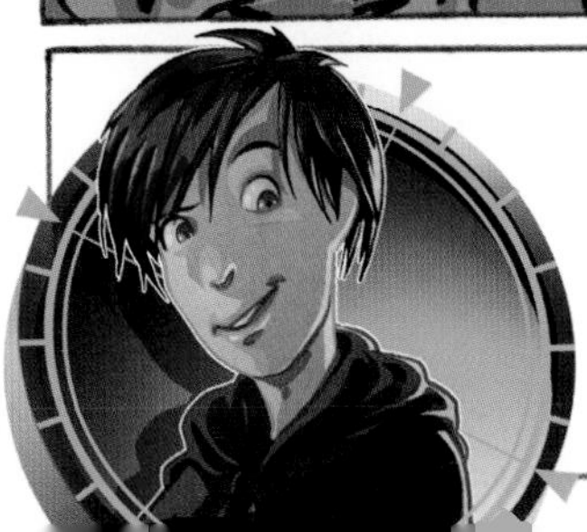

FLUX FACT

Claim jumpers were men who took over other miners' spots illegally and took them as their own spots to dig. "Jumping" happened on a regular basis. Disputes over claims could be violent but were usually settled by a chosen jury of miners.

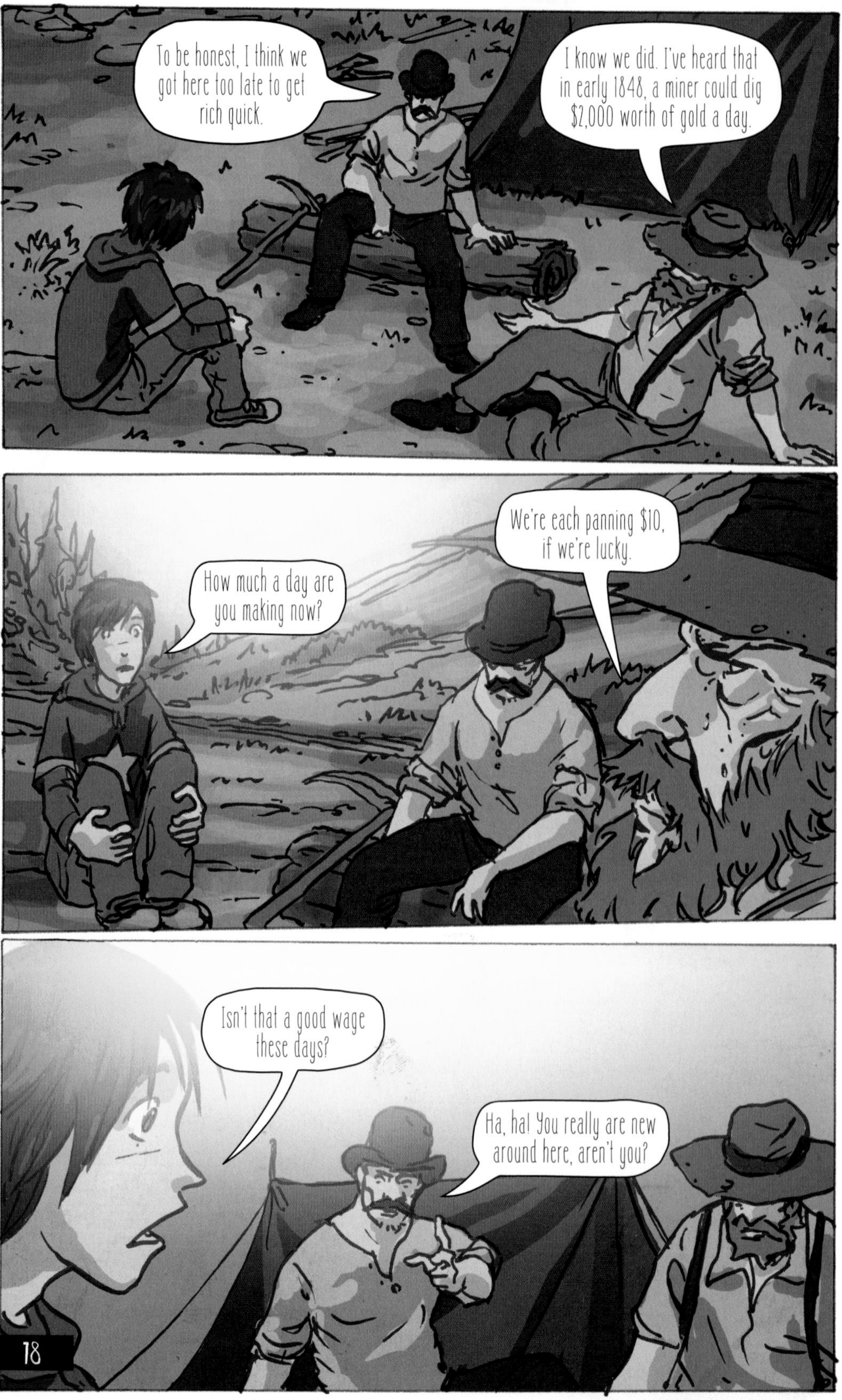

To be honest, I think we got here too late to get rich quick.
I know we did. I've heard that in early 1848, a miner could dig $2,000 worth of gold a day.
How much a day are you making now?
We're each panning $10, if we're lucky.
Isn't that a good wage these days?
Ha, ha! You really are new around here, aren't you?

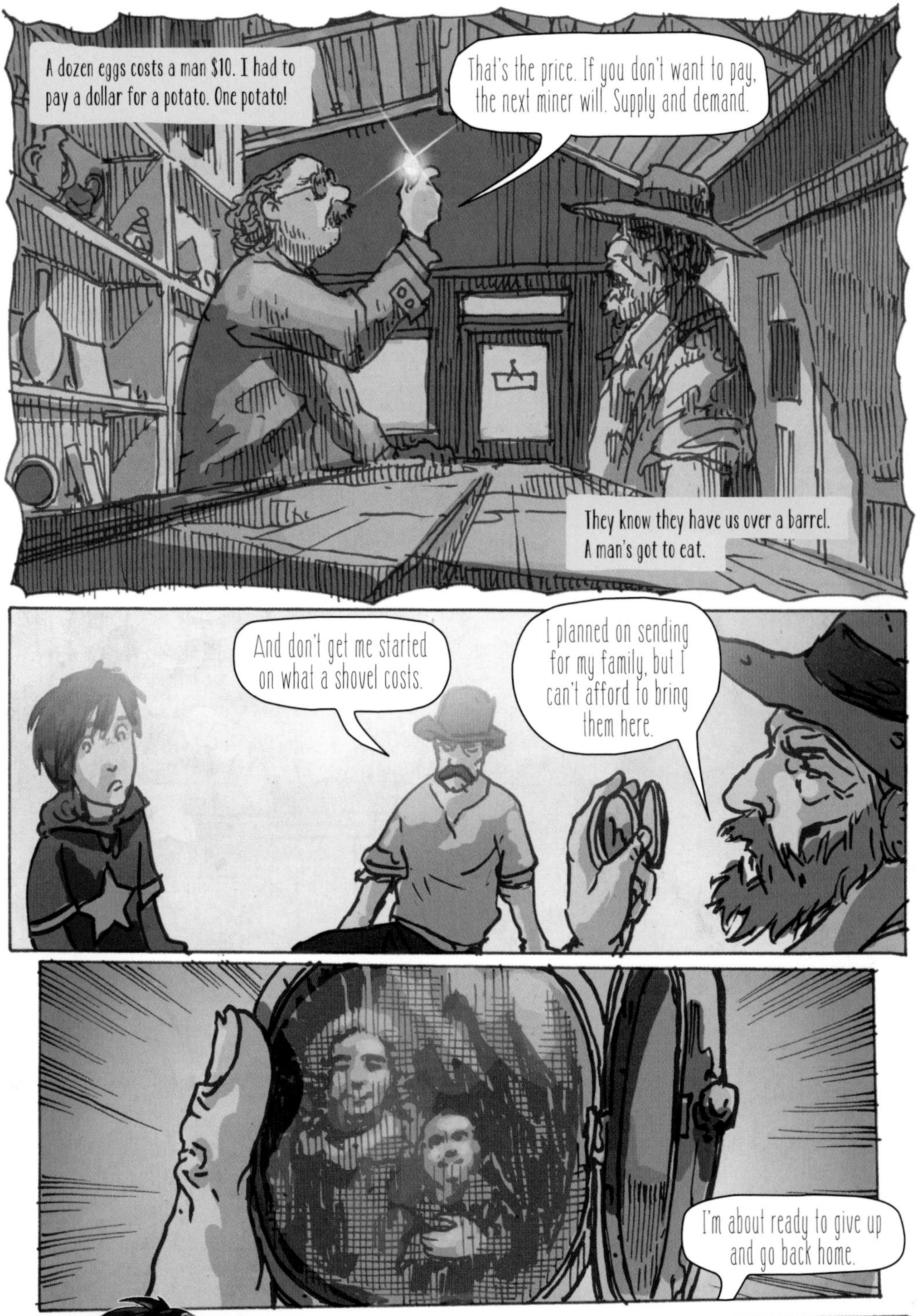
A dozen eggs costs a man $10. I had to pay a dollar for a potato. One potato!
That's the price. If you don't want to pay, the next miner will. Supply and demand.
They know they have us over a barrel. A man's got to eat.
And don't get me started on what a shovel costs.
I planned on sending for my family, but I can't afford to bring them here.
I'm about ready to give up and go back home.

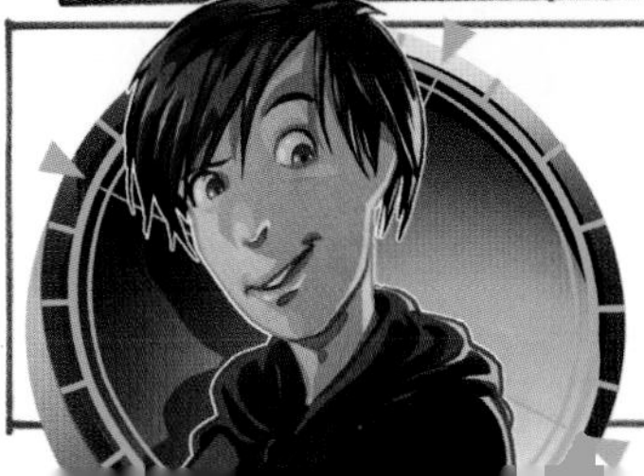

FLUX FACT

Limited supply and high demand led to high prices during the gold rush. Merchants knew miners needed tools for mining and food to eat. Miners had to pay whatever the merchants charged.

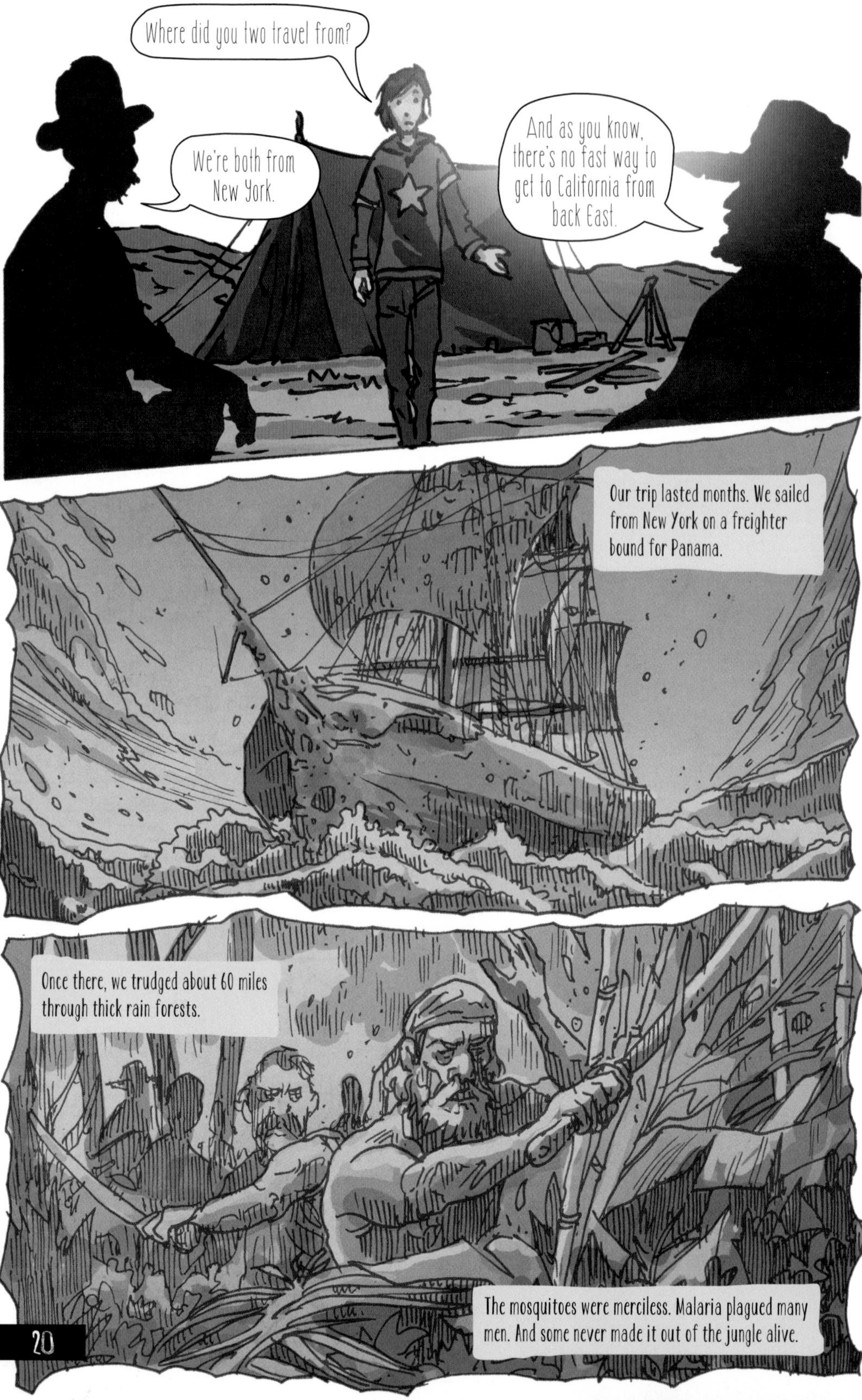
Where did you two travel from?
We're both from New York.
And as you know, there's no fast way to get to California from back East.
Our trip lasted months. We sailed from New York on a freighter bound for Panama.
Once there, we trudged about 60 miles through thick rain forests.
The mosquitoes were merciless. Malaria plagued many men. And some never made it out of the jungle alive.

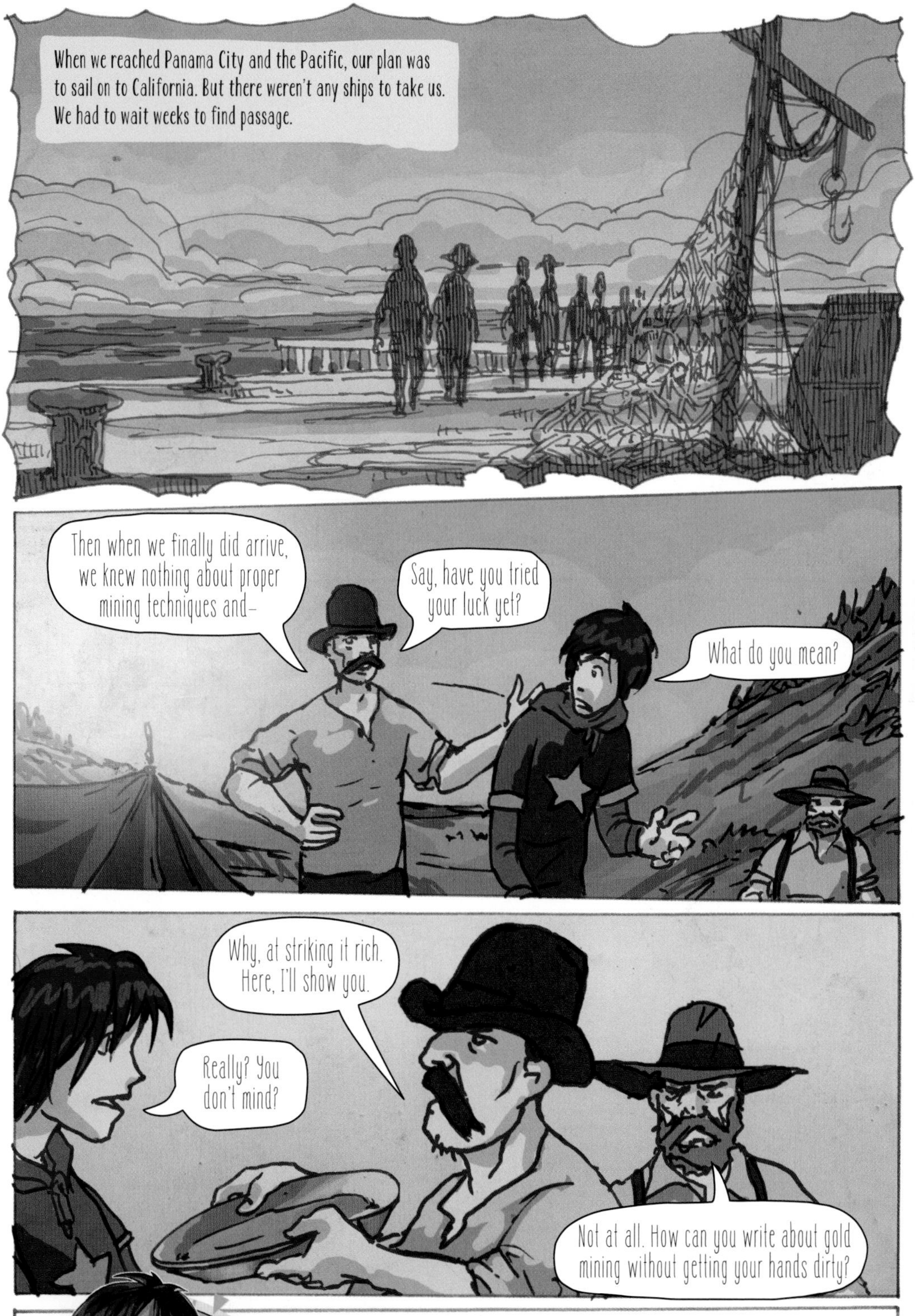
When we reached Panama City and the Pacific, our plan was to sail on to California. But there weren't any ships to take us. We had to wait weeks to find passage.
Then when we finally did arrive, we knew nothing about proper mining techniques and–
Say, have you tried your luck yet?
What do you mean?
Why, at striking it rich. Here, I'll show you.
Really? You don't mind?
Not at all. How can you write about gold mining without getting your hands dirty?

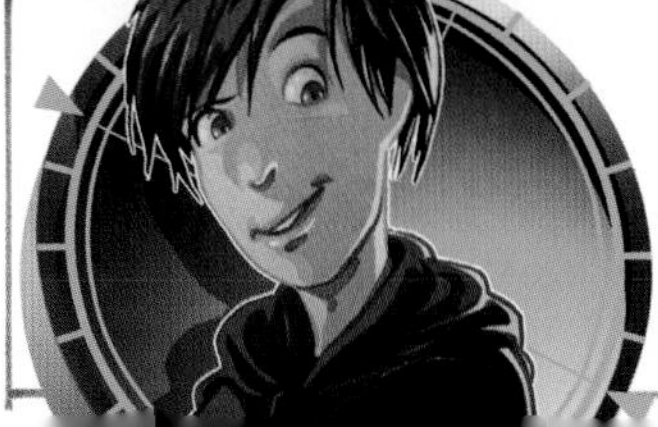

FLUX FACT

Although taking a boat was faster, most people traveled to California over land. On a good day, a covered wagon could travel 15 miles (24 kilometers). The whole overland trip often took five to six months.

CHAPTER FOUR
JUMPED!

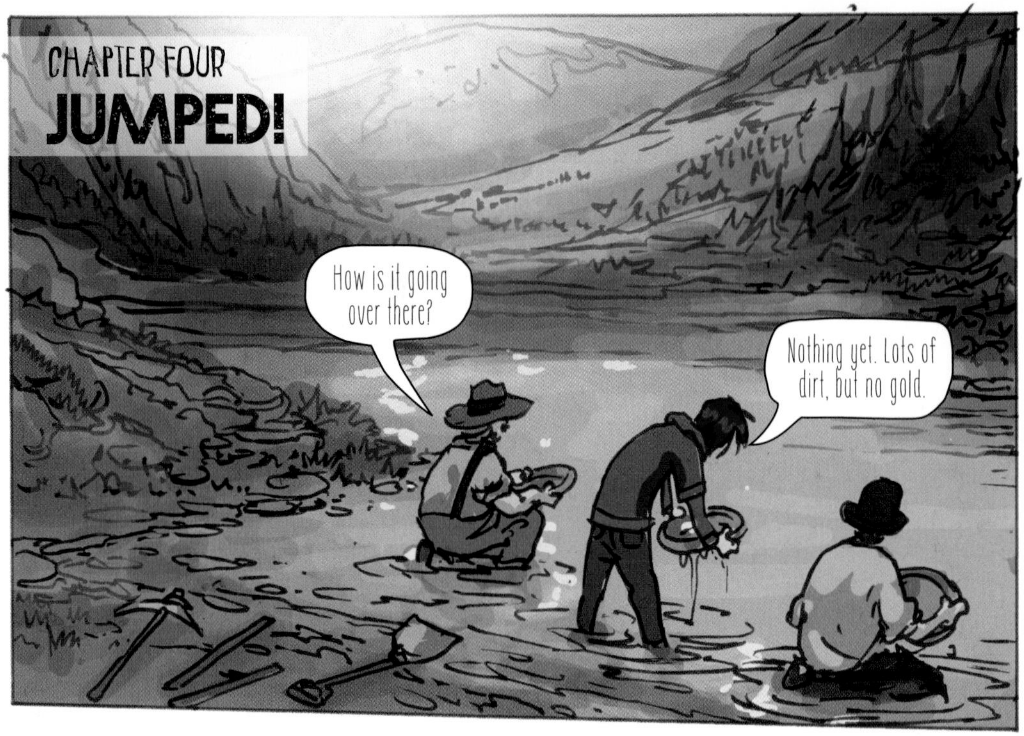
How is it going over there?
Nothing yet. Lots of dirt, but no gold.

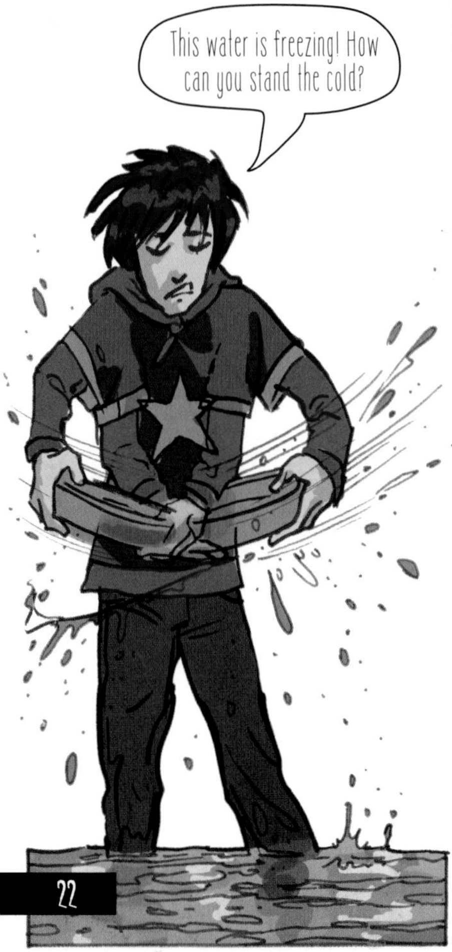
This water is freezing! How can you stand the cold?

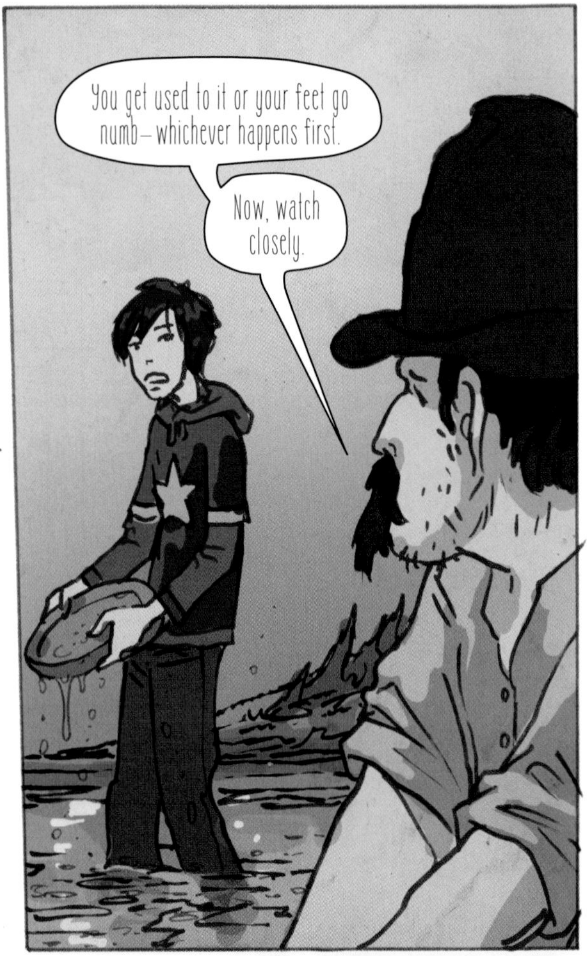
You get used to it or your feet go numb—whichever happens first.
Now, watch closely.

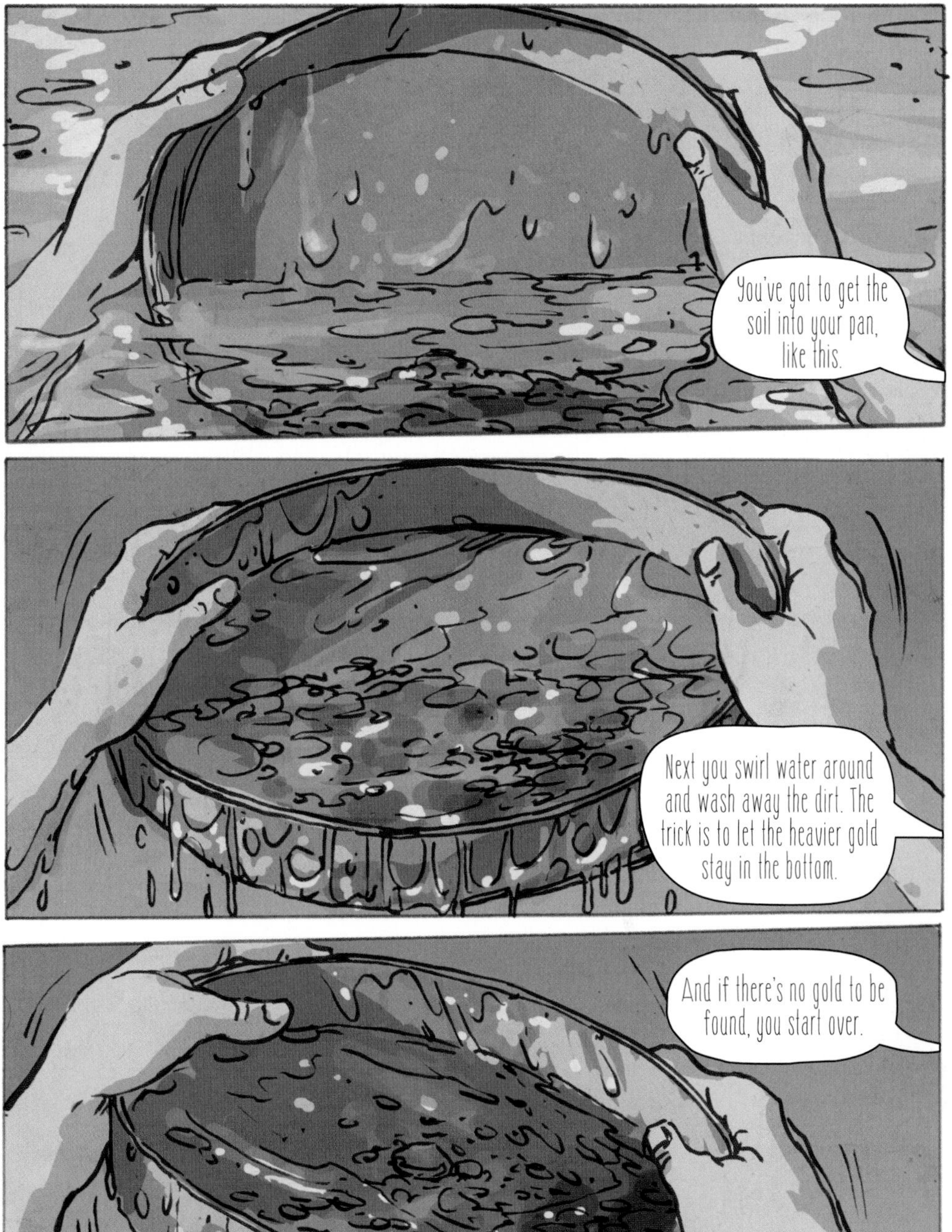
You've got to get the soil into your pan, like this.
Next you swirl water around and wash away the dirt. The trick is to let the heavier gold stay in the bottom.
And if there's no gold to be found, you start over.

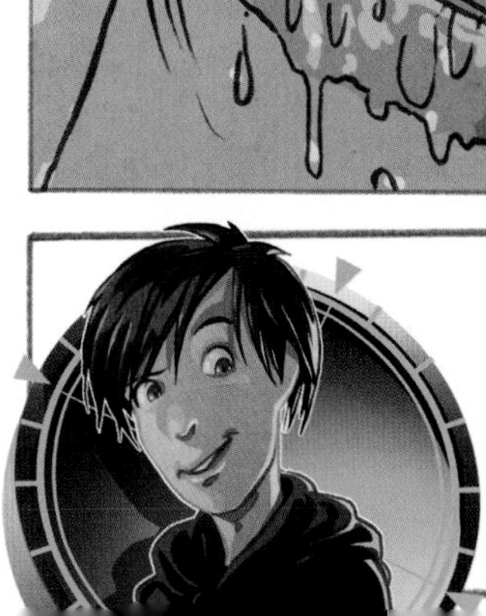

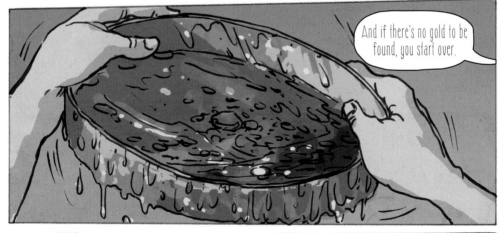

FLUX FACT

Panning for gold was the simplest way to mine, but it was also the slowest. A miner might go through a ton of dirt just for a single ounce of gold. To speed the process, miners developed wooden machines called cradles and Long Toms.

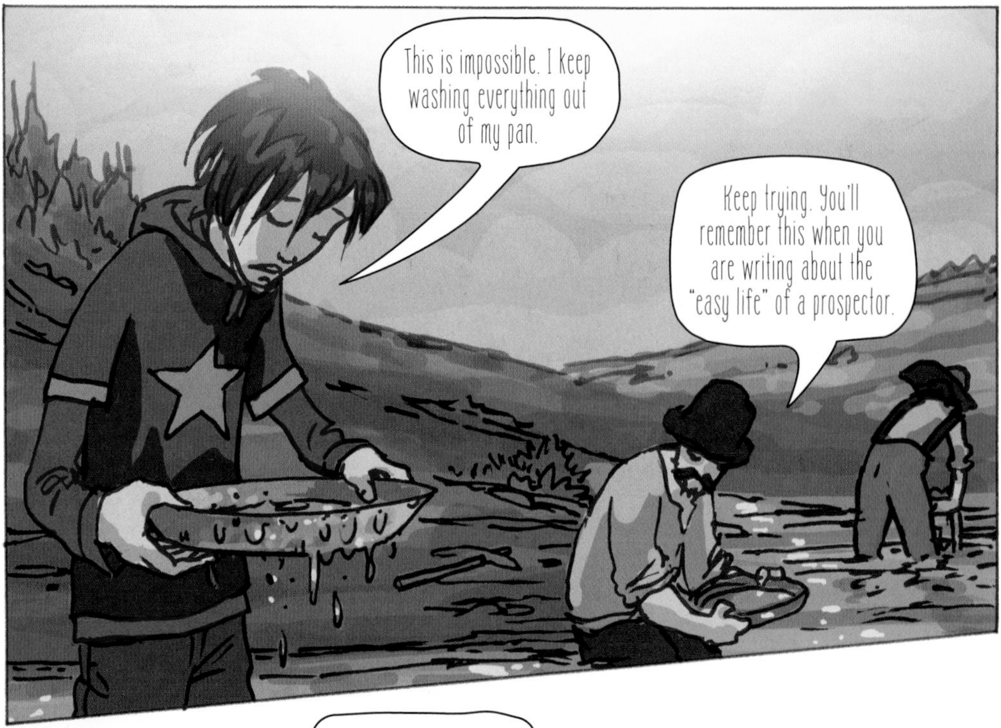
This is impossible. I keep washing everything out of my pan.
Keep trying. You'll remember this when you are writing about the "easy life" of a prospector.

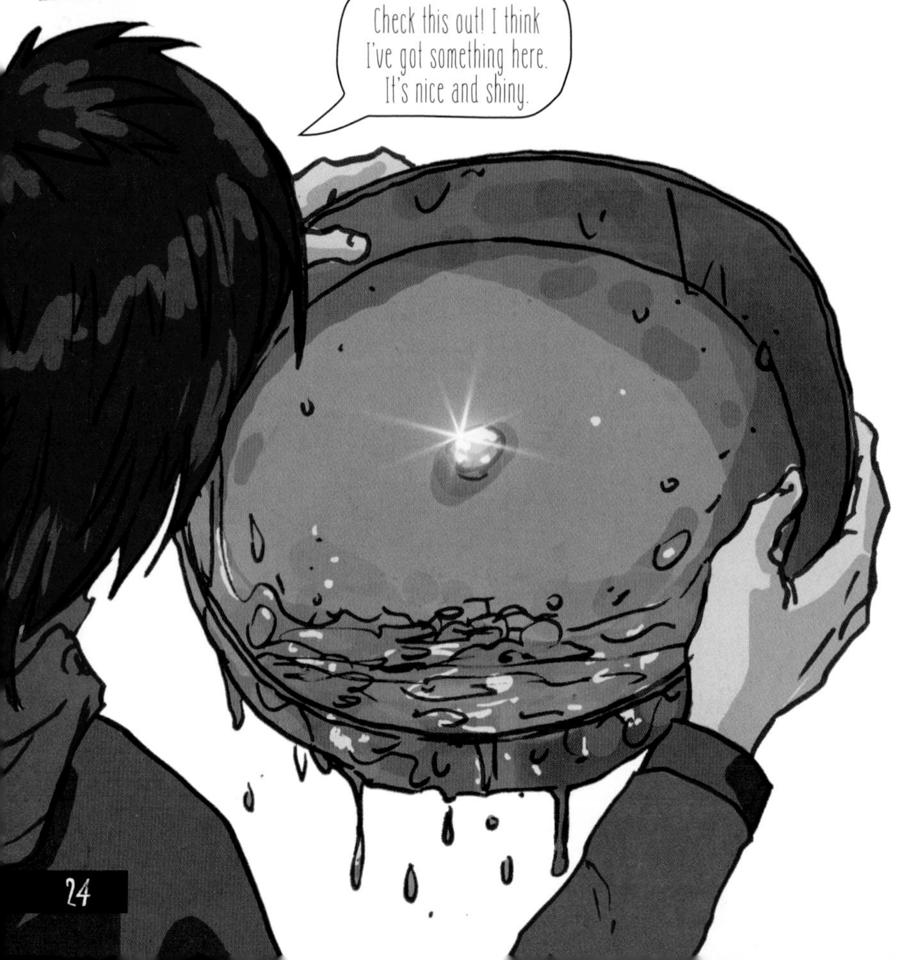
Check this out! I think I've got something here. It's nice and shiny.

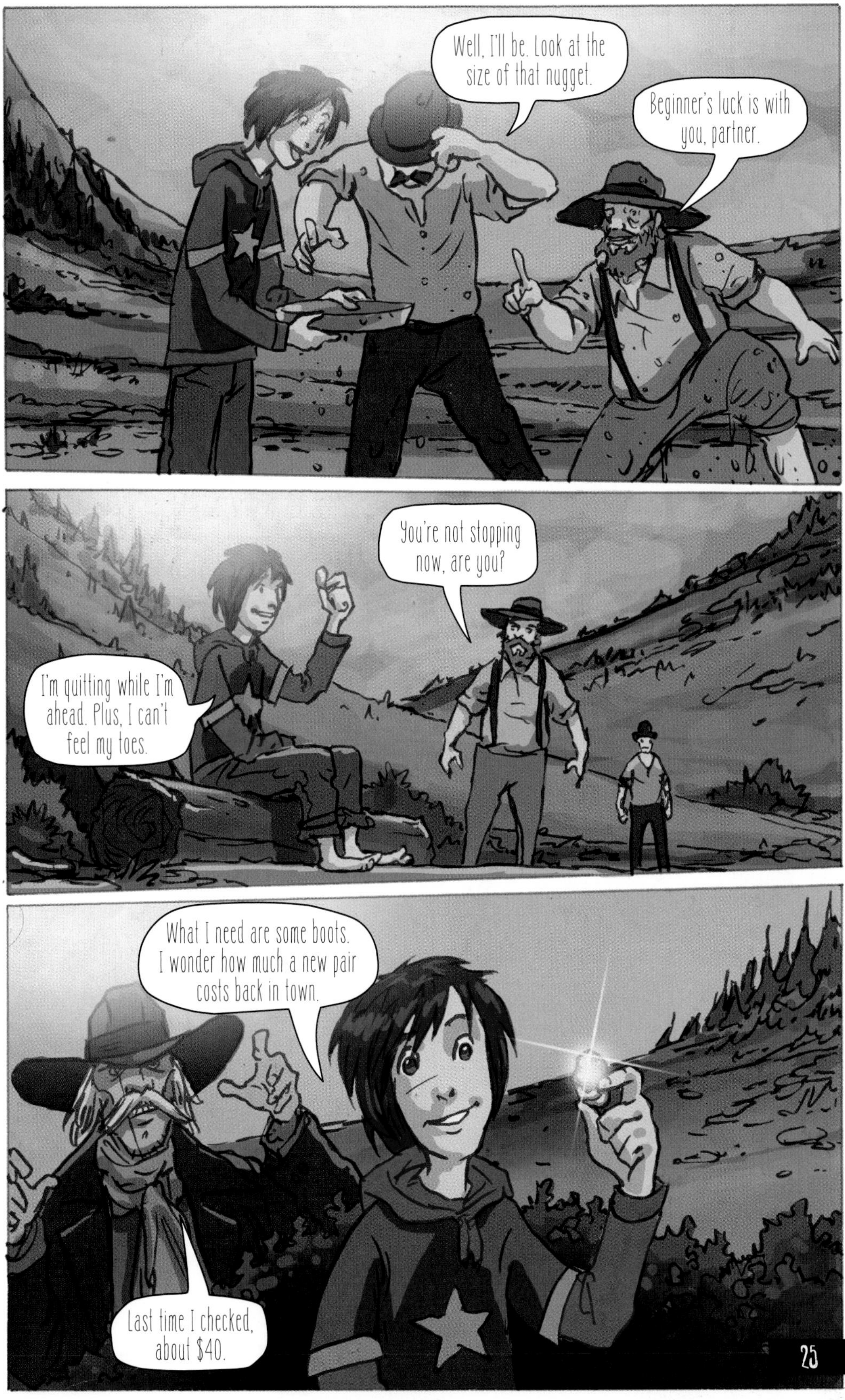
Well, I'll be. Look at the size of that nugget.
Beginner's luck is with you, partner.
You're not stopping now, are you?
I'm quitting while I'm ahead. Plus, I can't feel my toes.
What I need are some boots. I wonder how much a new pair costs back in town.
Last time I checked, about $40.

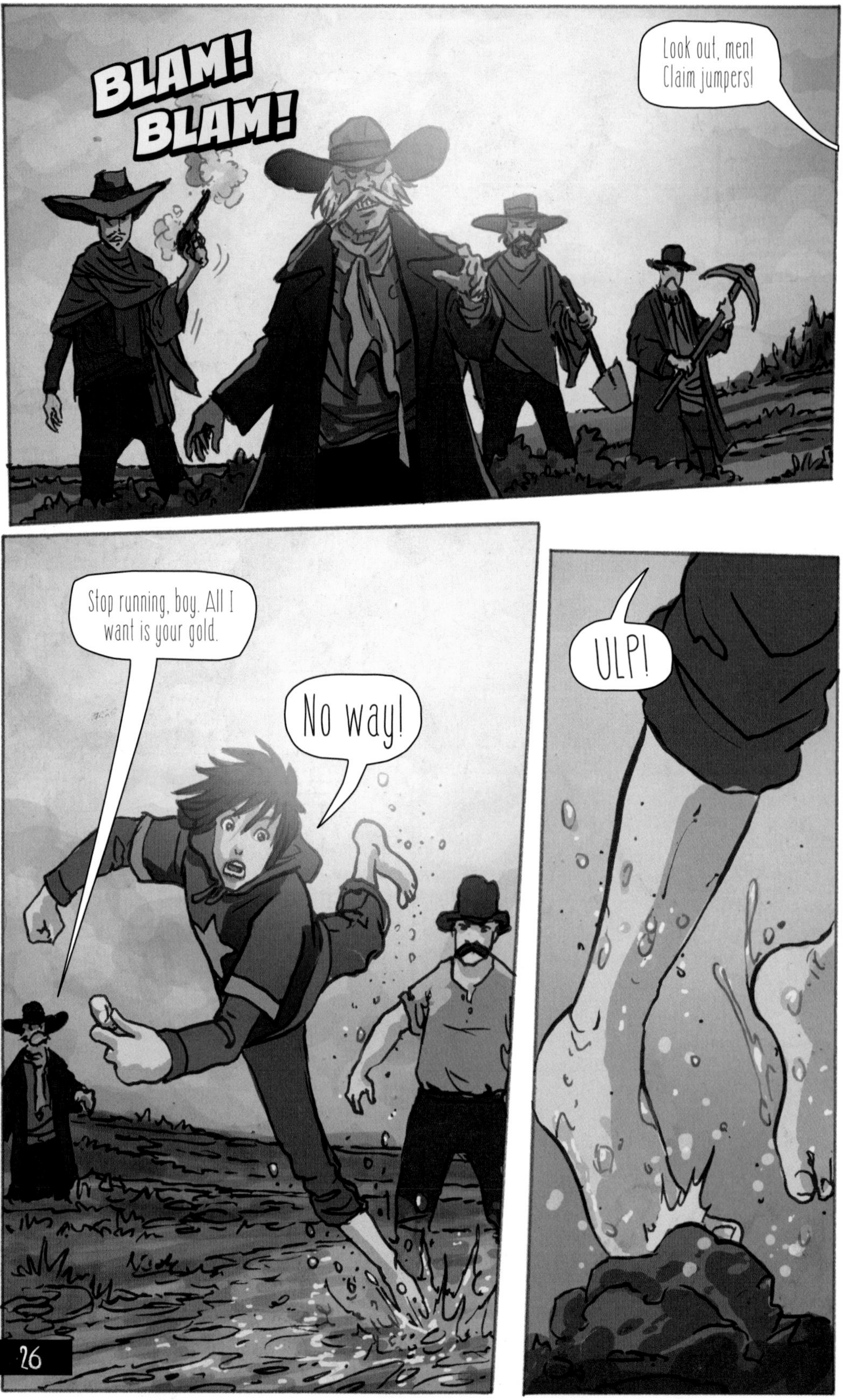
BLAM! BLAM!
Look out, men! Claim jumpers!
Stop running, boy. All I want is your gold.
No way!
ULP!

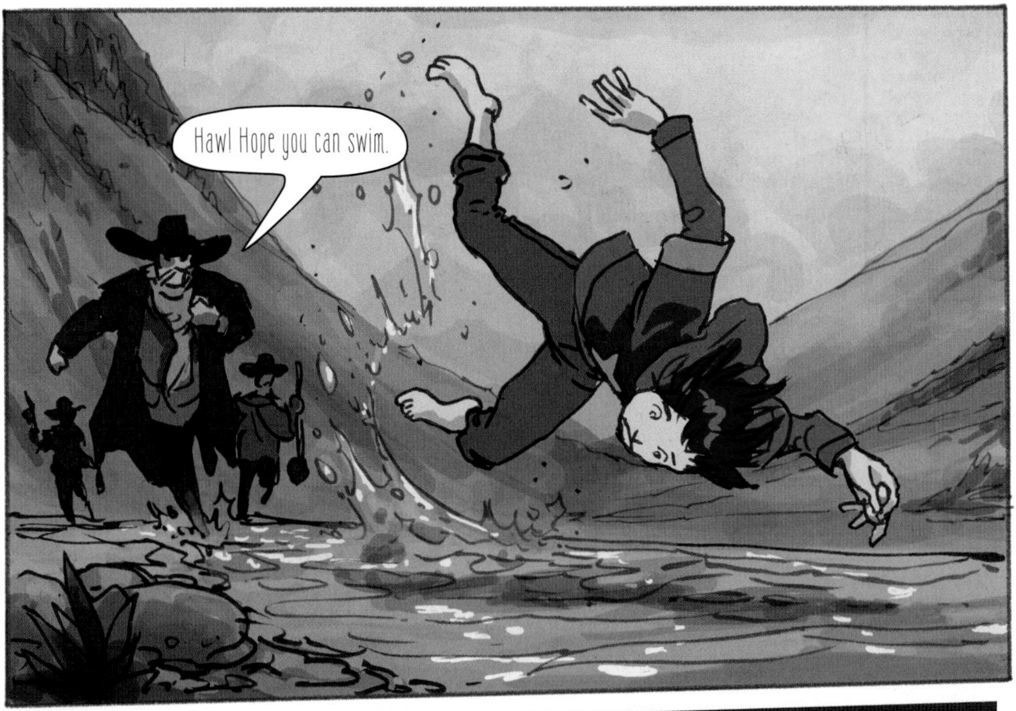
Haw! Hope you can swim.

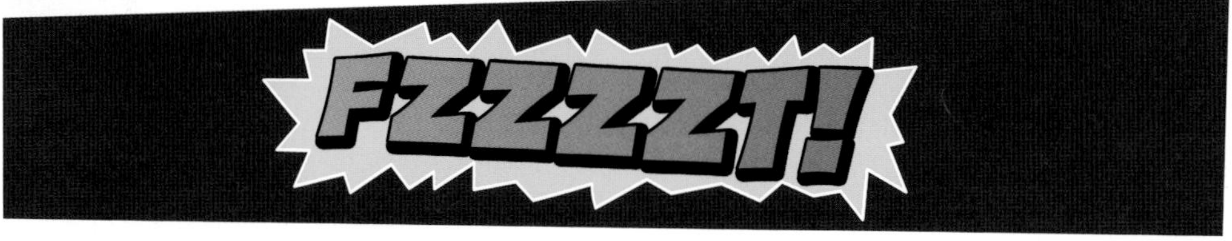
FZZZZT!

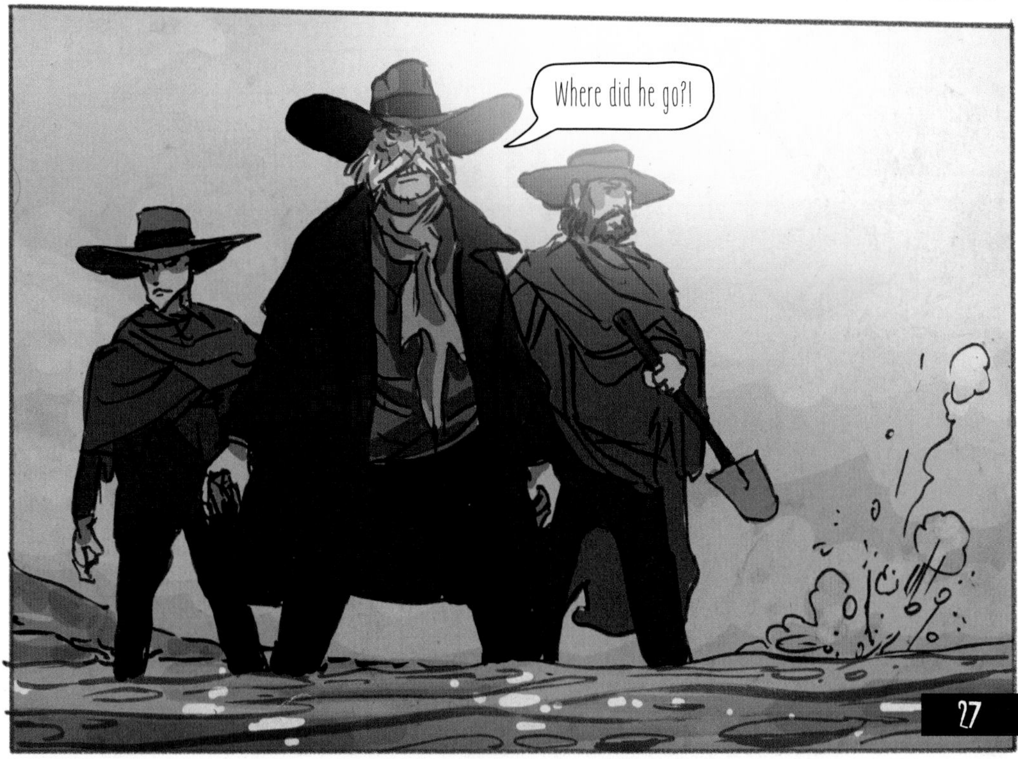
Where did he go?!

CHAPTER FIVE

BACK TO CLASS

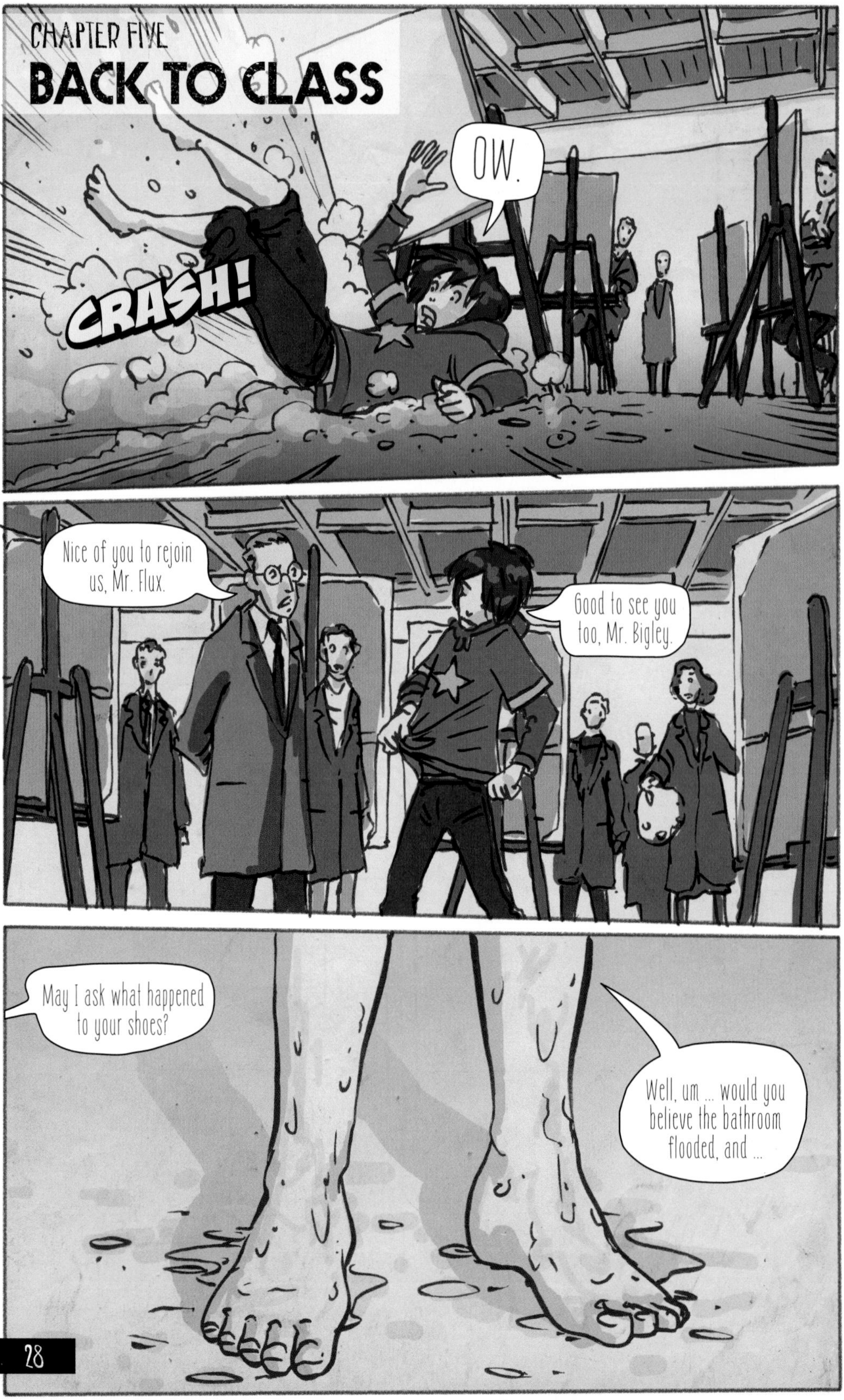
CRASH!
OW.
Nice of you to rejoin us, Mr. Flux.
Good to see you too, Mr. Bigley.
May I ask what happened to your shoes?
Well, um ... would you believe the bathroom flooded, and ...

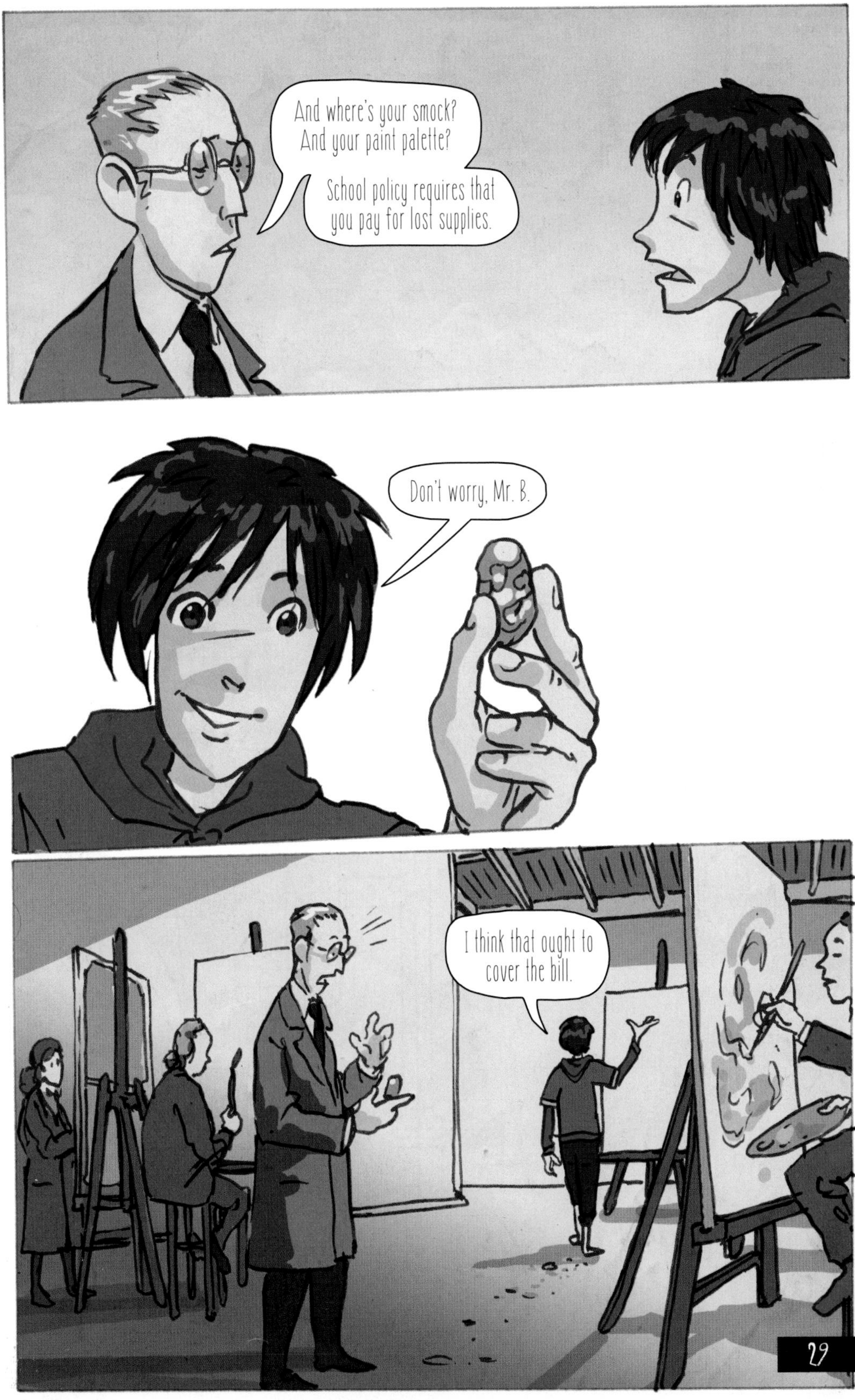
And where's your smock? And your paint palette?
School policy requires that you pay for lost supplies.
Don't worry, Mr. B.
I think that ought to cover the bill.

FLUX FILES

CRADLES

Gold miners used other tools besides pans. One of these was the cradle. Using a handle on the cradle, a miner could rock it while dumping dirt and gravel into the top. Buckets of water washed the debris down through a screen. The bottom part of the cradle caught heavier metals, including gold.

LONG TOMS

Another mining tool was known as a Long Tom. A larger version of the cradle, the Long Tom was between 8 and 20 feet (2 to 6 meters) long. A paddle wheel ensured a constant source of water. Three people were needed to operate this tool. One shoveled dirt. A second kept the water flowing. The third person rocked the device from side to side.

WOMEN DURING THE GOLD RUSH

Women also benefited financially from the gold rush. They could charge high prices for cooking meals, a skill many men in the mining camps lacked. Mary Jane Caples wrote of selling fruit pies for $1.25 and mince pies for $1.50 each. Another woman claimed she baked 1,200 pies a month. She wrote that she made $18,000 by selling them to miners.

SAM BRANNAN

The gold rush made Sam Brannan rich, but he wasn't a miner. After buying every mining tool in the region, he marked up the prices. A 20-cent metal pan was now available from Brannan for $15. In a little over two months, he made $36,000!

TRAVEL BY LAND

Traveling to California from the East Coast by land was a dangerous task that took months. Roughly one out of 10 travelers died along the way. Cholera was the number one killer, causing diarrhea and severe dehydration. Rufus Porter planned to fly 49ers west on propeller-driven balloons powered by steam engines. He advertised the expedition, but the ambitious plan never worked out.

MINING CAMP JUSTICE

Since California wasn't a state when the gold rush started, there were no laws in the mining camps. The miners had to establish their own. In some camps, a claim was on 10 square feet (1 square meter), and each person was allowed one. Taking someone else's claim, or "claim jumping," was common. Punishment for crimes was brutal. Small crimes were punished by a beating with a whip. For more serious crimes, the punishment was hanging.

WELLS, FARGO & CO.

In 1852 Henry Wells and William Fargo founded Wells, Fargo & Co. They opened for business in the gold rush port of San Francisco. The new bank bought gold and also offered express delivery of valuables. With this rapid start, the company went on to open offices in all of the other mining camps of the West.

POPULATION BOOM

Before the gold rush, California was largely populated by American Indians and European Christian missionaries. During the gold rush era, California's population increased from about 15,000 to more than 250,000. Only 60,000 residents were required for California to become a state, which it did on September 9, 1850. Without the 49ers, California's gain in residents would have taken decades, instead of just two years.

GLOSSARY

ABUNDANCE (uh-BUN-duhnss)—having plenty of something

CLAIM JUMPER (KLAYM JUHM-pur)—a person who steals land that belongs to someone else

JURY (JU-ree)—a group of people at a trial that decides if someone is guilty of a crime

LOCUST (LOH-kuhst)—a type of grasshopper that flies in huge swarms and eats and destroys crops

MALARIA (muh-LAIR-ee-uh)—a tropical disease people get from mosquito bites; symptoms include chills, fever, and sweating

PROSPECTOR (PROSS-pek-tur)—a person who looks for valuable minerals, especially silver and gold

PROSPERITY (prahs-PAYR-uh-tee)—doing very well or being a success

SAWMILL (SAW-mil)—a place where people use machines to saw logs into boards

TERRITORY (TERR-uh-tor-ee)—an area under the control of a country

TRESPASS (TRESS-pass)—to enter someone's private property without permission